Advance Praise for *New Ways to Engage Parents*

"Long a leader in the field, Professor Patricia Edwards reinforces the fact that education is a shared responsibility of home, school, and community. She presents scores of practical ideas and resources to enable educators to involve all parents in their children's education. This includes details on effective open house nights, new technologies for two-way communications between teachers and parents, designs for student-led parent–teacher conferences, and more."

—Joyce L. Epstein, director, Center on School, Family, and Community Partnerships and National Network of Partnership Schools (NNPS), Johns Hopkins University

"Finally a book that brings partnering with parents into the 21st century! Edwards begins this book with a heartfelt personal history and rationale for why developing parent–teacher partnerships is so important, and she then packs it with detailed, engaging, and practical suggestions for bringing parents and teachers together so that children have rich and relevant opportunities to learn. This is a book teachers will want to keep at their fingertips!"

—Jeanne R. Paratore, professor and program director, Literacy and Reading Education, Boston University

"This book moves beyond traditional parent involvement approaches to focus on specific strategies for engaging all families in partnerships to support their students' learning. With lots of practical suggestions and resources, this book will help readers immediately update, expand, and enhance their parent-engagement efforts."

—Laurie Elish-Piper, acting dean, distinguished teaching professor, and presidential engagement professor, College of Education, Northern Illinois University

"*New Ways to Engage Parents* is loaded with practical advice that can help educators engage with families in respectful and culturally sensitive ways. With strategies ranging from teacher notes to classroom blogs, every teacher should find a wealth of ideas for building home–school partnerships."

—Deborah Wells Rowe, Peabody College, Vanderbilt University

"Patricia Edwards provides an action-oriented framework and proven strategies for school administrators, teachers, coaches, and teacher educators to create partnerships with families that are linked to student learning goals. This is not a one-size-fits-all approach. Edwards helps us think critically about outmoded practices that often distance diverse parents from schools and shows us how to replace them with up-to-date strategies for engaging contemporary families."

—Judy Carson, manager for school-family-community partnerships, Connecticut State Department of Education

NEW WAYS TO ENGAGE PARENTS

Strategies and Tools for Teachers and Leaders, K–12

Patricia A. Edwards

Foreword by Catherine Compton-Lilly

TEACHERS COLLEGE PRESS

TEACHERS COLLEGE | COLUMBIA UNIVERSITY

NEW YORK AND LONDON

Published by Teachers College Press, 1234 Amsterdam Avenue, New York, NY 10027

Copyright © 2016 by Teachers College, Columbia University

Cover photos (top to bottom): Courtesy of Bruce Washburn (www.flickr.com/ btwashburn); courtesy of enfad; courtesy of Rose Physical Therapy group (all under creative commons attribution licenses); and Steve Debenport, Getty Images.

Figure 5.1 reprinted with the permission of SEDL, an affiliate of American Institutes for Research (AIR). The Afterschool Training Toolkit is a product of the National Partnership for Quality Afterschool Learning, an initiative funded by the 21st Century Community Learning Centers program of the U.S. Department of Education, Office of Academic Improvement and Teacher Quality Programs in the Office of Elementary and Secondary Education. The Partnership is led by SEDL, Austin, Texas, and includes the National Center for Research on Evaluation, Standards, and Student Testing (CRESST) at the University of California, Los Angeles; the Mid-Continent Research for Education and Learning (MCREL), Aurora, Colorado; the Northwest Regional Educational Laboratory (NWREL), Portland, Oregon; SERVE, Greensboro, North Carolina; American Institutes for Research (AIR), Washington, DC; and WGBH Educational Foundation, Boston, Massachusetts.

Library of Congress Cataloging-in-Publication Data is available at loc.gov

ISBN 978-0-8077-5671-3 (paper)
ISBN 978-0-8077-7389-5 (ebook)

Printed on acid-free paper
Manufactured in the United States of America

23   22   21   20   19   18   17   16   8   7   6   5   4   3   2   1

This book is dedicated to my grandparents Tate and Callie Plummer and to my parents, John and Annie Kate Edwards, for their guidance and love and for developing in me the need to care about other people. Also, I thank my grandparents and parents for helping me set and reach my goals and turn my research on school, family, and community partnerships into treasured real-life experiences.

Contents

Foreword

On a recent visit to her home, Ms. Cicero, a Mexican American parent who is deeply committed to the education of her three daughters, consulted with members of our research team about how to read her daughter's new middle school report card. The report card featured a confusing array of numbers and letters as well as long lists of categories and subject areas. The key to the report card was at the bottom of the second page in notably small print and in English. Our research team has been working with Ms. Cicero and her daughter for the past 6 years. As part of that work we visited homes and talked to parents about school. Lupita had just started middle school. She had moved from a school in which the children were taught to read in English to a middle school where bilingual children like Lupita were instructed in both Spanish and English. When asked, Ms. Cicero was confused about the differences between these two programs. For a mother who left school at age 12 in a country where education was unavailable to children who could not pay tuition or afford school uniforms, being the parent of children attending American schools was confusing. While Ms. Cicero was thrilled at the after-school activities, the range of available courses, and the resources provided by the school, she often elicited help from us when we visited to talk about Lupita's experiences with reading and writing.

Ms. Cicero is an advocate for her daughters. She provides them with books, checks on their homework, and seeks people who can help her to decipher the papers that they bring home from school. Ms. Cicero believes that our visits are helpful to her daughters; they provide an opportunity to ask questions, seek clarification, and receive confirmation from people who know about American schools. In *New Ways to Engage Parents*, Patricia Edwards recognizes the strengths that parents like Ms. Cicero bring to their children's literacy learning. Edwards provides educators with strategies and insights to support teachers in connecting with parents in ways that honor parents' knowledge and experiences while helping them to negotiate their children's schools.

In Edwards's world, there are no generic parents. Parents are people, each bringing a unique set of passions and practices to their children's upbringing and education. In my own work, I have focused on temporality and the ways that being in time affects how we make sense of the world. Edwards also situates sensemaking within time. She locates her understandings about education within a rich family legacy of African American educators and within African American communities. In diverse communities, as in all communities, parents bring their own histories of schooling that feature both accomplishments and frustrations.

As Edwards reminds us, parents and family members bring their "ghosts" with them to school. These ghosts are the instantiation of historical discrimination, and their presence can contribute to the trust or distrust that parents may bring to schools and classrooms. Friendly or unfriendly, invited or uninvited, these ghosts accompany parents as they enter schools and interact with teachers. Edwards's ghost metaphor is a particularly apt way of highlighting the histories that are too often invisible to teachers and all too visible to parents. In becoming aware of family strengths and being sensitive to the challenges they face, educators can begin to confront the ghosts.

In order to serve parents who bring diverse experiences to their children's classrooms, Edwards maintains that we need data—information that will help us to understand their experiences and perspectives. She asks us to learn about the communities we serve. What types of jobs do people have? What cultural groups are represented? What languages are spoken? What barriers do parents face as they strive to support their children in school? These are data that, as Edwards argues, will "broaden teacher and administrator understanding of families and provide a window into the lives of the families and children in their school" (p. 4). They are data that promote insight rather than assumption and focus on people rather than test scores. Data are collected to reveal disparities and identify spaces of possibility for children and their families. Data that matter take parents' voices seriously and respond to their concerns.

According to Edwards, working with diverse families also requires examining our own experiences with school, literacy, and learning. As educators, we must open our eyes to the biases we carry and the assumptions we make. Assumptions must be addressed as educators move toward becoming culturally responsive. Once we move beyond assumptions and are able to hear the voices of parents and children, then we can begin to build trust—a trust that can tame the unruly ghosts of the past.

In addition to examining our own histories as learners, educators must recognize the strengths of the communities they serve. Edwards invites educators to identify community organizations and resources that teachers can access to support children and families. She provides suggestions on how parent–teacher conferences can be crafted to support parents in making sense of students' progress, and she outlines how technology—including texting, Skype, Google Hangouts, school websites, Twitter, and blogs—can be used to communicate with parents. Suggestions are provided for working with parents who are learning English, families dealing with incarceration, young mothers, parents who struggle with English literacy, parents of children with disabilities, and unemployed parents. Each of these circumstances brings a unique set of challenges that families must navigate as they support their children in school.

As I write this Foreword, I consider how this book pushes the field forward. While decidedly among the most important literacy scholars of our era, Pat Edwards locates progress on the ground—in the work of educators and in the operation of schools. Specifically, Edwards invites educators to consider the data that matter to children and communities. No, this book is not about test scores. It is about people's lives and the lessons that people can teach us about their worlds and about education. It is about Ms. Cicero and a million other parents, each bringing their unique situations, passions, and histories to their children's schools. It is my hope that this book inspires teachers to seek ways to make schools more equitable and caring spaces for all children.

—Catherine Compton-Lilly

Preface: My Community, the Families, the School

> Literacy and education are valued and valuable possessions that African-American families have respected, revered, and sought as a means to personal freedom and communal hope, from enslavement to the present.
>
> —Vivian L. Gadsden, "Literacy, Education, and Identity Among African-Americans: The Communal Nature of Learning"

This quote reflects my family's view about education, and I am fairly sure the views of other African American families. Other examples of Black families with high educational values are found in works such as *Maggie's American Dream: The Life and Times of a Black Family* (Comer, 1988) and *Gifted Hands: The Ben Carson Story* (Carson, 1990). I often heard my parents, John and Annie Kate Edwards, say that

John and Annie Kate Edwards (the Author's Parents)

education has always been an equalizer for the African American community.

My own educational values were instilled by my parents, who always made school a top priority in our family. They had their own parents as models. For example, my maternal grandfather, Tate Plummer, organized a school for African American children in the early 1900s, and his brother, Elzee, was the first teacher at the Plummer School. The school catered to sharecroppers' children and children who lived on plantations. The Plummer School was located in Albany, Georgia, the county seat for Dougherty County. In his classic book *The Soul of Black Folk*, renowned scholar Dr. W.E.B. Dubois (1903) portrayed Dougherty County as a place where vast ignorance festered untouched. My grandfather recognized this and worked tirelessly to change it.

My grandmother, Callie Robinson Plummer, shared a story with me that was later confirmed by my 92-year-old elementary school principal, Mr. Erasmus Dent, in a December 2012 interview. Mr. Dent had been my mother's childhood friend, and he had actually attended the Plummer School. He and my grandmother indicated that my grandfather had asked the Albany mayor and the superintendent of

Tate Plummer (the Author's Grandfather), Founder, Plummer Colored School

Tate Plummer started a school in Albany, Georgia, in the early 1900s to provide African American children with an opportunity for an education.

schools to provide school transportation for sharecroppers' children and children who lived on various plantations. The answer was "no."

My grandfather owned property and houses where 22 sharecropper families lived on his land. He, along with the help of two of his brothers, Elzee and Tucker, and Elzee's wife, Ella, worked to make the Plummer School a success for African American children. My grandfather and his close family members recognized, like John Dewey (1902), that "What the best and wisest parent wants for his child that must the community want for all its children. Any other ideal for our schools is narrow and unlovely; acted upon, it destroys our democracy" (p. 7). Even though things were not democratic during these times, my grandfather was not focused on democratic ideals; he simply wanted to make the best out of an unfair and unjust situation and to give African American children the opportunity to receive an education.

My grandmother's brother, Baily Robinson, along with his wife, Aretha, realized the importance of an education for their visually impaired son. They enrolled him in a state-supported school where he received a formal music education and learned to read, write, and arrange music in braille. Their son, Ray Charles "Robinson," went on to an extraordinarily successful music career. Education also played an important role in my uncle Joseph Plummer's life, as he was the first in my family to graduate from college and he went on to become the first Black principal in Milwaukee, Wisconsin. Uncle Joseph's alma mater, Albany State University, became my choice for college, and it was also the institution recognized by Ray Charles, as he provided a sizable contribution.

In the Deep South during the 1950s and 1960s, the African American community was an institution to which African American parents and children looked for strength, hope, and security. More important, the African American community set both a floor and a ceiling on achievement and educational attainment for its members. Billingsley (1968) describes five key interactions in which elders socialized younger community members:

> In every aspect of the child's life a trusted elder, neighbor, Sunday school teacher, schools, or other community member might instruct, discipline, assist, or otherwise guide the young of a given family. Second, as role models, community members show an example to and interest in the young people. Third, as advocates they actively intercede with major segments of society (a responsibility assumed by professional educators)

to help young members of particular families find opportunities which might otherwise be closed to them. Fourth, as supportive figures, they simply inquire about the progress of the young, take a special interest in them. Fifth, in the formal roles of teacher, leader, elder, they serve youth generally as part of the general role or occupation. (p. 99)

Lightfoot (1978) echoed a similar message:

Black families and communities have been settings for cultural transmission, survival training, moral and religious instruction, role-modeling, myth-making, and ideological and political indoctrination. But very little of this "informal" education has been systematically documented by scholars because it has been considered distracting and divergent from the formal schooling of black children. (p. 129)

Growing up in a mid-sized city in southwestern Georgia, I remember vividly that the family, the school, and the community contributed to the educational achievement of African American children. I entered school a few years after the 1954 U.S. Supreme Court landmark decision *Brown v. Topeka Board of Education*, which declared segregation in education unconstitutional. I grew up in a stable, close-knit neighborhood where I knew many eyes watched me, and my mama always knew when I deserved praise or misbehaved and should receive punishment. My elementary school principal and most of my teachers lived in my neighborhood. Consequently, there were many opportunities outside of school for my principal and teachers to talk with my parents about my progress and behavior in school. My principal, teachers, and neighbors, as well as my parents, shared and reinforced similar school and family values.

Before school desegregation, African American parents had a place in the school. They felt comfortable coming and going to the school at their leisure. The faces of teachers and administrators were familiar to them because, in many instances, the teachers and administrators were their friends, neighbors, and fellow club and church members. In other words, there were numerous opportunities for teachers and administrators to develop social networks outside of school. It did not matter if parents were rich or poor, educated or uneducated; they could voice their concerns, opinions, and fears about their children's educational achievement, and teachers and administrators listened and responded.

For many African American parents whose children attended segregated schools, parent involvement connoted active participation, collaboration, and cogenerative discussions with teachers and administrators. It meant African American parents had some control of the school and school systems that helped shape the character and minds of their children. For example, teaching personnel were accountable to the community and, therefore, had to both teach effectively and communicate with parents if they wanted to maintain their jobs. Parents' views were strongly considered as a warning to teachers who were viewed as ineffective teachers. The school's curriculum was relevant to the life experiences and needs of African American children, thus, in turn, providing motivation to learn. African American children developed self-worth and dignity through knowledge of their history and culture and through the examples or role models provided by community leaders and teachers. African American parents had control through coalition. The administration maintained continuous communication with African American parents and developed with these parents a structure that included them formally and informally in the governing of the schools. African American parents could exert influence to protect their most precious resources, their children. This involvement assisted schools in providing a more relevant education for students.

My mother was president of the parent–teacher association (PTA) throughout my entire 6 years of elementary school, which meant that my sister and I had to attend all of the PTA meetings. In fact, we provided the entertainment at these monthly meetings as we offered musical selections on the piano and xylophone. We also assisted Mama with fundraising activities. As I reflect back on these PTA meetings, I can remember hearing Mama *tell* parents: "Education is the key to a better life and brighter future for our children. We, as parents, must help the teachers help our children in school. We want our children to have a better life than we have right now." My mama's commitment to bridging the gap between home and school has shaped my understanding of what it means for families to be involved in their children's educational lives.

I want to make the point here that segregation was unequal, unfair, and wrong, and it meant that the textbooks, equipment, and supplementary materials were often outdated and inferior compared to what was provided at all-White schools. Despite this, African American schools often implemented a curriculum that reflected high standards and compelled their students to exceed expectations in order to be successful in the "real world." Additionally, African American parents had a sense of value and pride because the African American principals and teachers in these segregated schools made them feel needed, wanted, and included in the business of the school.

Hawkins (1970) argues, "When schools are too largely removed from a sense of immediate responsibility to their clientele, education is in danger. The institution becomes the master rather the servant of those it teaches" (p. 270).

My hometown is not the same today, and one might comb the country and likely not find even a handful of places where schools, families, and communities are so entirely and supportively entwined. However, the hopes of today's educators and parents for our nation's increasingly diverse populations of children—including urban, rural, and various ethnic and immigrant groups, as well as the shamefully large population of children living in poverty—have not changed. They are tied to the education of their children and the dream that their children will have a good, productive life filled with opportunities. The difference is that today's parents often send their hopes to school with their children and remain on the outside. They need to be brought in. There is a need for doors to be reopened in both directions, and, as my mother said, parents need to help the teachers to help their children. Teachers and administrators need to help parents know how to do that. We cannot return to a time when it was common for parents, students, and teachers to live, shop, and worship together in the neighborhoods, grocery stores, and churches, so our challenge is to create structures and spaces for new communities of parents, teachers, and principals to come together with the mutually understood purpose of educating children. We need to create the sense of personal respect and two-way accountability between parents and schools that made my segregated school function so well. When parents or caregivers are reluctant to engage in school functions, teachers and administrators need to find the root causes of hesitations and address them.

School professionals bring a wealth of background experiences that assist in their formation of ideas about how parents might be approached and encouraged within school settings. Schools have rapidly changed, as demographics are in a continual shift. Just as populations change, ideas about how to encourage and work with parents also need to evolve: School officials and teachers must think of new and creative ways in which to welcome, encourage, and involve parents within their schools, and they cannot take a "one-size-fits-all" approach. Educators will find that *New Ways to Engage Parents* is an excellent resource for examining varied ways to approach parents. In this book I provide a framework to help administrators, teachers, literacy coaches, and teacher educators engage the wide range of parents in today's schools. This book is meant, as JoBeth Allen (2010) said, "to be lived by a community and to create that community, bringing together educators and families" (p. 3).

The book's eight chapters are designed for use by a study group or whole faculty, by teacher educators, and in graduate and undergraduate courses in teaching and school leadership. Chapter 1 guides school leaders and teachers to take a stark look at changing community demographics in the 21st century. Chapter 2 points to the implications of those changes for teacher and administrator understanding and provides strategies to develop home–school relationships, including with the parents of preschool children. Chapter 3 highlights ways to maximize contact opportunities with parents, and Chapter 4 explains how to take advantage of technology in teacher–parent communication. Methods of encouraging parental leadership and involvement in schools in meaningful ways are the focus in Chapter 5, and Chapter 6 emphasizes the importance of understanding constraints of parents and the need to meet them halfway. Chapter 7 describes how to overcome the "ghosts" that linger in schools, and the final chapter provides a new vision of how to encourage parents to take an active role in their children's school lives.

Resources for this book are available on the Teachers College Press website, tcpress.com. Readers are alerted to each resource by a cross-reference in a text chapter.

Although I am an African American teacher educator and researcher, I feel that my experiences can be generalized to all communities. This book is intended for all who are interested in learning how to involve a wide range of families in our nation's classrooms and schools irrespective of their ethnic identity or socioeconomic level. It is my hope that this book will serve as a road map for expanding and broadening readers' knowledge base for working with diverse families and children.

Acknowledgments

Writing a book can be a lonely task. I used to wonder how a person could be so self-disciplined as to spend hundreds of hours confined to a computer and a room cluttered with piles of resource materials. I find it is fatal to dwell on such matters before starting, but now that the book is complete, I rejoice at having reached the end of the tunnel. I can now luxuriate in contemplating the details of my journey.

My many lonely hours of writing were made infinitely more bearable by my good friend and acquisition editor, Jean Ward. From the moment I conceived the idea of this book to the present, Jean has been of invaluable assistance—providing suggestions, sending materials, helping with the outline, summarizing reviews, and generally being supportive. I think she also did some prodding, but she was so charming and diplomatic that I welcomed it. I also acknowledge with much appreciation the thoughtful suggestions made by the reviewers who read the first and second drafts of this manuscript. Their contributions helped make this a better book.

During the last few weeks of writing, when all of the elements seemed too disorganized to pull together in order to make the deadline, I reached out to a network of classroom teachers and former doctoral students who came to my rescue. Jane Bean-Folkes, a teacher/practitioner and assistant professor; Jackie Sweeney, Nicole Martin, and Maria Selena Protacio, former Michigan State doctoral students; and current Michigan State doctoral student Laura Hopkins took time from their busy schedules to edit content, develop charts and graphs, and help with formatting. Nina Hasty, Kathleen Davis, and Krista Hunsanger also took time from their busy schedules to help with this project. Nina Hasty, also a former Michigan State doctoral student, provided numerous examples of how to communicate and work with a wide range of families and children. Kathleen Davis, a 1st-grade teacher/literacy coach, co-owner of the Literacy Ladies LLC, and a master's student in two of my classes, provided several examples of blogs, screenshots, websites, and examples of how she and other teachers at her school communicate with families and children. Krista Hunsanger, 2nd-grade teacher/reading specialist and co-owner of The Literacy Ladies, LLC, provided blogs and screenshots and helped collect release forms from parents. This book would never have happened without their encouragement, their joy in the project, their absolute commitment to my work, and their unending patience, advice, and constructive feedback. There is no way to adequately acknowledge the value and extent of their contributions.

Finally, this book would not have been possible without the loving support of my two sisters—Callie R. Hall and Sandra Johnson. I would like to thank Catherine Compton-Lilly for so graciously agreeing to write the Foreword, and I am very thankful for the patience and expertise of John Bylander, Nancy Power, and Jamie RasmussenTeachers College Press.

Although the task of writing can be lonely, I have been warmed by the knowledge that these people cared enough to lend support above and beyond the ordinary. I want them to know I shall be forever grateful.

NEW WAYS TO ENGAGE PARENTS

CHAPTER 1

Your School's Reality

When schools were an integral part of stable communities, teachers quite naturally reinforced parental and community values. At school, children easily formed bonds with adults and experienced a sense of continuity and stability, conditions that were highly conductive to learning.

—James P. Comer, "Home, School, and Academic Learning"

Some time ago, I had the opportunity to interview my 1st-grade teacher, Mrs. Hattie Taylor, for an article on African American parent involvement in schools before and after school desegregation (see Edwards, 1993a). In this interview, Mrs. Taylor talked about the teacher–parent relationship in my segregated elementary school:

Parents were teachers' right-hand partners. Whatever the teachers did was supported fully by the parents and no questions were asked. . . . All I had to say to a parent was "I need your support" and that meant any type of support—field trips, chaperones, making refreshments, serving as room mother, helping their children with homework . . . even if parents could not help their children, they found a way to make sure their children did well in school. I don't know whether parents asked a neighbor or an older child to help the younger one, but I do know the child was helped. (pp. 352–353)

There still remain segregated schools in some communities throughout the United States, but many of these communities are not close-knit like the town I grew up in during the 1950s and 1960s. Just as our school communities have changed, few teachers and administrators would disagree that the face of our nation is changing, and nowhere is the change more evident than in public school classrooms. In a 2012 report of the Center for Public Education, Ron Crouch made revealing observations about the U.S. population: (1)

1

it is growing older, (2) it is growing more diverse, and (3) it is growing rapidly.

These shifting demographics bring transformations into the nation's
social fabric and economy, and public schools are at the vanguard of
change. School leaders are challenged to meet the needs of a student
population that includes increasing numbers of minorities and English
language learners (ELLs). A first step in meeting that challenge is to re-
consider the role of the school in light of changing demographic realities.

Once teachers understand the complexities of our changing society, especially in regard to diversity, they may then understand how
those changes affect the teaching that takes place in their classrooms.
Studying their schools and communities to build a better understanding of their population is a good start. This is important not only for
teachers but for districts as a whole. When district administrators/
leaders research and recognize the demographic characteristics of
their school's population, this information can be an integral part of
district decisions about issues such as open houses, curriculum nights,
conferences, district communication, and professional development
for staff. The following sections provide a road map to assist district
administrators and teachers with gaining a better understanding of
their school's population.

COMPREHENSIVE PLANNING BEGINS WITH GOOD DATA

When a school district experiences population growth, the most no-
ticeable change is the need for the district to increase facilities and staff
to accommodate the increasing number of students enrolled in the
schools. However, the increase in school population is generally a result of changing demographics in a district. These changes can include
families who have moved from suburban or urban areas to new housing developments in what was a previously a rural setting and families
who have come from school districts with different school and community cultures. Whether it is planning for facilities or for educational
services, school leaders need to start with good answers to questions
about the families who live within their communities. The following
questions provide an indication of the kinds of data schools need:

- What is the occupational breakdown of the parents by
  percentage (i.e., blue-collar jobs, office jobs, teaching jobs,
  food service jobs, etc.)?

- What is the average education level of the parents?
- What is the median family income?
- What is the average household size?
- What are the family profiles (as indicated by the percentages of each of the following: one parent, two parents, blended families, doubled-up families)?
- How many children under age 5 live in the community?
- What is the birth rate?
- What is the population breakdown by race or ethnic group?
- What languages do families in the school's community speak?
- What percentage of the population is foreign born or speaks a language other than English at home?
- What percentage of children in the community attends preschool?
- What barriers exist for parents in enrolling children in preschool?

Many of the answers to these questions can already be found in data that school districts collect through avenues such as PowerSchool and other data-management systems. Schools gather some of this information when students enroll, and some additional material may be found within community resources. Databases as shown in Figure 1.1 can provide a wealth of information regarding the community such as data on

Figure 1.1. Sample Graph of Parental Occupations

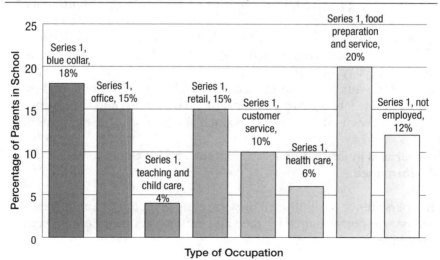

parent workplaces (see Figure 1.1), sibling ages, socioeconomic levels, ethnicities, gender, languages spoken, number of parents in the home, and so forth. While schools can learn a great deal from data-collection tools, they are not enough; analysis and discussion are also needed. For example, analyzing the data to determine the percentage of students in grades 1 to 3 who speak a home language other than English would lead administrators and teachers to discuss alternative ways to communicate with these families and children.

The further questions in the sections below can guide school leaders in gathering more detailed data. The answers to these questions will help broaden teacher and administrator understanding of families and provide a window into the lives of the families and children in their school. Crouch (2012) suggests areas that have to be addressed and poses questions for discussion centered around changing demographics, disparities in achievement, limited educational skills, and lifelong learning.

Increase in English Language Learners

Changing demographic patterns may bring more non-English speakers into your schools—and your neighborhoods:

- What are the English proficiency levels of parents in your community?
- What languages/cultures are represented among your ELLs? (See Figure 1.2 for an example of data from one elementary school in Michigan.)
- Are your programs for ELLs designed to develop proficiency in reading and comprehending academic English in addition to everyday speech?
- Are your programs staffed with highly qualified bilingual or ELL teachers? Are your parent-involvement and community-outreach efforts geared to reach the parents of these students?

Disparities in Educational Attainment and/or Behavioral Performance

The persistence of significant disparities in educational attainment and behavioral performance by race and ethnic group presents a serious challenge:

- What do your data show about disparities between the
  academic performance of different racial, ethnic, and
  socioeconomic groups? What is your school doing to address
  disparities?
- Do gaps exist between these subgroups in the areas of
  behavioral performance and possibly behavioral referrals?
  How are these influencing academic performances?
- Have you established mentoring, tutoring, and dropout
  prevention programs for students?
- Have you involved parent organizations, community groups,
  and others in the effort?
- How have you communicated with parents and the
  community to inform them of gaps and student needs?

Some districts have systems in place for analyzing data such as academic and/or behavioral disparities between subgroups. Some schools use data-management systems, such as School Wide Information System (SWIS) or system databases, to keep track of behavioral referrals and gaps between subgroups. School breakdown reports based on race and ethnicity in regard to student behavior can be printed and used for staff analysis. Student behavior is often a major factor in

Figure 1.2. Languages Represented Among Roosevelt Elementary School's English Language Learners

Arabic	Jin	Russian
Bengali	Kannada	Spanish
Burmese	Korean	Sundanese
Cajun	Malay/	Swahili
Cantonese	Indonesian	Tagalog
Creole	Malayalam	Tamil
Dakota	Mandarin	Telugu
Dutch	Marathi	Thai
Inuit	Min Nan	Turkish
Italian	Navajo	Ukrainian
French	Nepali	Urdu
German	Oriya	Uzbek
Hakka	Pashto	Vietnamese
Hausa	Persian	Wu
Hindi	Polish	Xiang
Hmong	Portuguese	Yupik
Japanese	Punjabi	
Javanese	Romanian	

learning in public schools—schools can discuss how they can improve behaviors (decrease referrals) in order to improve instructional time and, therefore, student academic success.

In examining their data, if schools notice that the majority of their referrals are for one racial subgroup, this information affects their standing with the state as a possible focus school. It can also guide staff professional development and conversations about why this might be happening. Questions to be addressed include the following: Are we unfairly giving referrals to one racial group more than another but did not realize it before looking at real data? How can we stop this? Or, is this a group of students that is not feeling supported/represented in school activities, literature, and so forth and therefore is struggling behaviorally or academically? It is important for administrators and teachers to look at data in terms of thinking about how to better serve these students. This is different from looking at data and then creating stereotypes.

Effectiveness of Educational Programs

As jobs get smarter, those with limited education and skills are getting left behind:

- What can our schools do to ensure that high school graduates have the skills they need to contribute to a global economy?
- Are we encouraging female and minority students to enroll in upper-level science and mathematics courses and recognizing students for academic as well as athletic accomplishments?
- Do we have plans and programs to support and motivate boys, who are dropping out in greater numbers than girls?

Support for Lifelong Learning

The combination of slow growth in the workforce, an aging population, and changes in technology puts new emphasis on retraining and lifelong learning as the nation works to stay competitive:

- What role can your schools play in expanding learning beyond the K–12 years?
- How is the integration of 21st-century literacies and technology being prioritized in your school district?

- What technological infrastructures and goals are in place that will provide students with the opportunity to compete in the ever-changing workforce?
- How involved and knowledgeable is your community in understanding the importance of the integration of 21st-century literacies and technology? Are community members involved in decisionmaking and supporting options to improve these areas such as through bond proposals?

Like the rest of society, public schools must continually reinvent themselves in a changing world that presents new and greater risks to the families and children that they serve.

CREATING A DEMOGRAPHIC PROFILE

The data school leaders have gathered can be used to create a demographic profile (see Edwards, 2004, 2009). A *demographic profile* is a composite description of the parent community that exists in your school building, as well as in individual classrooms. The benefits of constructing a demographic school/classroom profile are as follows:

- Allows teachers to develop tailor-made, parentally appropriate activities
- Helps teachers take a look at the history of parent involvement at the school level
- Allows teachers to determine whether parental involvement has been effective or not
- Gives teachers a way to pinpoint where problems may be occurring
- Allows teachers to interact with families in ways that are specific to their needs
- Provides teachers with an in-depth look at the strengths of a family/community
- Gives teachers real data and removes the guesswork/judgments/assumptions about families
- Allows teachers to connect to families on a grade-by-grade basis (see Edwards, 2004, 2009)

In order to provide differentiated instruction to students, parental input is very important. However, unless teachers understand the cultural, linguistic, and socioeconomic diversity that exists within their school communities, they may have difficulty reaching out to parents. It is important that teachers understand the definition of parent involvement. According to Carol Ascher (1988), the term *parent involvement* "may easily mean quite different things to different people" (p. 109). In a broad sense, parent involvement includes home-based activities that relate to children's education in school. It might also include school-based activities where parents actively participate in events that take place during the school day. *Parent involvement* is the participation of parents in every facet of children's education and development from birth through adulthood, accompanied by the recognition that parents are the primary influence in children's lives (Edwards, 2009).

Just as *parent involvement* has multiple meanings, so does the term *parent*. The term can refer to all those who are involved in a child's education because we recognize that other adults such as grandparents, aunts, uncles, stepparents, and guardians may carry the primary responsibility for a child's education and development. In this book, *parent* includes any adult who plays an important role in a child's upbringing and well-being.

Since many teachers today may live outside of the districts in which they teach, in order to learn more about the communities in which they work, they might first begin with examining the area in which the school is located as well as the special school identity. Principals and teachers might make it a point to take short walks within the community and visit the neighborhoods, stop in local grocery and convenience stores, observe the various businesses in the neighborhood, and note storefront closures and "for rent" signs. This might provide a feel for neighborhood interaction and activity. Are people greeting one another, stopping to talk, or is there a lot of anonymity? What might be noticed about families and their lives? What activities can teachers observe that might be incorporated into classroom practices? This information might begin to present a picture of the families who live in the neighborhood and the lifestyles they value. Sweeney (2012) noted that "in order to know students, families and their communities, teachers need to hone their abilities to deeply notice in ways that assist them in recognizing opportunities that allow them to teach in the most fair and equitable ways" (p. 3). This might refer to noticing not only inside of schools but also within the situated communities. To assist with a deeper level of noticing, teachers and administrators might first begin by taking a closer look at the community as teachers and administrators consider the type of school and its setting, as well as the special programs offered by the school. To begin the profile, jot down the characteristics of your school and community. (See Figure 1.3 for three examples of demographic profiles, using fictitious data, of schools in urban, suburban, and rural settings; for examples of profiles of specialized schools, see Resource 1.1, tcpress.com.)

Digging deeper and continuing the creation of a demographic profile can assist teachers and administrators with knowledge about their schools, students, families, and teachers.

Who's in Your School?

As indicated, schools continue to evolve with demographic change. Teachers can use knowledge about their school demographics to assist them in their work. Upon recognizing the characteristics of the school, teachers can begin to look more specifically at the school descriptors. For example, what is the free and reduced lunch rate for the school? The free and reduced lunch rate might provide insight into the challenges some families face. The higher the free and reduced lunch rates, the lower the income for families within the school community. Many times this information may be found on the school district website or on the state department of education website. Eligibility guidelines may be found on the U.S. Department of Agriculture website (www.fns.usda.gov/cnd/ Governance/notices/iegs/IEGs.htm). They correspond to the federal poverty guidelines.

This information can be vital in identifying barriers to student success. If teachers realize that students' basic needs are not being met (i.e., they may be receiving free lunches at school but are not getting proper meals at other times and/or on the weekends), they may want to work to support these needs before expecting participation in rigorous academics. One example might be a district's participation in programs such as Blessings in a Backpack, where bags of food are packed and provided to students every Friday afternoon in

Figure 1.3. Examples of Creating a Demographic Profile and Appropriate Activities

School Type Characteristics	Knowing the Neighborhood	Families Within the School	Getting to Know Your School Community Projects
Urban: Relatively high rate of poverty (measured by free and reduced-price lunch data) Relatively high proportion of students of color Relatively high proportion of students who are limited English proficient learners Designated as a high-need or a Title 1 school (U.S. Department of Education provides supplemental to meet the needs of at-risk and low-income students) Classroom averages 35+ students	Many apartment complexes, tall buildings, great infrastructures, sports venues, many neighborhood stores that sell food and many churches—in close proximity, public transportation, many abandoned buildings, heavily developed dense areas with businesses, unkempt parks, and recreation venues	Low-skilled workers High unemployment rates Minority—African Americans, Hispanics/Latinos	*For all communities:* Scavenger hunt of certain facilities: Stores, first responders, banks, recreation facilities, hospitals, worship facilities Community service weekend: clean up parks, fields; paint parks; have a fundraiser (walk/run); volunteer at a shelter/soup kitchen Pass out clothing/food at the school for the community Have a fun day for the community to interact with school/staff and explore what they have to offer Workshops for community members to help them understand the resources within the community
Suburban: Middle-class and affluent families Classroom averages 25+ students	Many more colleges, shopping malls, higher-quality private homes, businesses, recreational facilities, and markets Larger homes that are not very close in proximity, well-kept neighborhoods	Some skilled workers Lower unemployment rates More professionals, college graduates	
Rural: Majority of student population is White or Native American; population of African Americans, Hispanics, Asians, or other races/ethnicities is small High levels of poverty and low income Relatively large number of students have Individualized Educational Programs Students are transported over a great distance	Homes on acres of land, farms, animals	Strong relationships and interactions of people within the community Agriculture as a prevalent source of income Generations of families remaining in the area Less populated	

order to ensure basic needs are being met over the weekend. In one small midwestern rural school district, all students who receive free and reduced meals at school also qualify to participate in this program. Families of these children are offered participation and have to formally accept by signing paperwork. Each week different volunteers within the community show up to pack the bags of food. On Fridays, bags are delivered to each school and are discreetly placed in student backpacks. Each bag contains enough food for the student to have each meal needed over the weekend (see Figure 1.4).

Teachers might also want to explore the cultural demographics of the school. What percentage of the school population is dominated by one particular culture? Are there historical tensions that exist

Figure 1.4. A Project That Serves the School and Community

Members of a varsity basketball team pose next to boxes of food after volunteering to pack the bags of food for needy students within their district. Volunteerism like this creates a powerful spirit of helping one another within the community.

between the different cultural groups in the community and school? How might you analyze the cultural demographics to assist with the quest to connect with parents?

What Do Your Families Look Like?

- Are the families small in size? Large? Rich? Poor? Immigrants? Refugees?
- How does knowledge about families assist teachers/ administrators in their quest to involve families?
- How is this knowledge being used to help families feel welcomed, valued, and needed? This is important to consider—many times districts "connect" with families through digital and written communication, but these families may not feel welcome, valued, and needed within the school building. Making this happen can encourage more parent involvement.

The school demographics can provide much information regarding income and statistics based on the cultural makeup, but teachers need to dive deeper into that information. For example, are the language learners in your classroom from an area outside of the United States? If so, are they immigrants or refugees? Are they proficient readers in their first language? Having that knowledge will assist you in connecting with parents and, ultimately, in determining how you will address the students in your classroom. Also, knowing the parents' cultural background provides you with insight into the cultural and linguistic capital that families have to offer (Moles, 1996). If teachers recognize parents' special talents, they might think of ways to integrate those talents into the classroom. You can record the information you discover in the last two columns of the chart in Figure 1.5.

What Do Your Teachers Look Like?

The changing demographics of students and families provide a challenge for U.S. teachers, as 83% are White (NCES, 2009); further, the typical teacher is monolingual and female and grew up in a suburban or rural area in a lower- or middle-class family (Feistritzer, 2011). Gather information on teacher characteristics following the example in Figure 1.6.

Figure 1.5. Demographic School Profile

	Characteristics	No. of Students	Percentage of Students
Sex	Male		
	Female		
Ethnicity	African American		
	Asian		
	Caucasian		
	Hispanic/Latino		
	Native American		
	Other		
Mother's level of English proficiency	Comfortable reading English		
	Comfortable speaking English		
	Comfortable understanding English		
Father's level of English proficiency	Comfortable reading English		
	Comfortable speaking English		
	Comfortable understanding English		
Mother's level of education	Some high school		
	High school graduate or equivalent		
	Some college		
	College graduate		
	Graduate/professional degree		
Father's level of education	Some high school		
	High school graduate or equivalent		
	Some college		
	College graduate		
	Graduate/professional degree		

Figure 1.5. Demographic School Profile (continued)

	Characteristics	No. of Students	Percentage of Students
Employment	Mother employed full-time		
	Mother employed part-time		
	Mother unemployed		
	Father employed full-time		
	Father employed part-time		
	Father unemployed		
Student's living situation	Lives with both parents		
	Lives with mother		
	Lives with father		
	Lives with grandparent(s)		
	Lives with other guardian		
	Doubled-up families in the home		
	Lives in homeless or abuse shelter		
Language spoken at home	English		
Form of transportation to school	Bus		
	Walk		
	Dropoff		
Additional data	Receive free/reduced lunch		
	Frequency of move in/move out		
	Distance between home and school		

Figure 1.6. An Example of What Your Teachers Look Like: Bayman City School

Position (No. of Teachers per Grade)	Teacher's Gender/Race/Age (in Years)	Years Taught	Educational Status	Area Teacher Grew Up/Lives In: Urban, Suburban (Sub), or Rural	Parents' Educational Background	Race of Students
K (1)	F/W/29	5	Master's	Sub/Sub	Both–college graduates	All AA
1 (2)	F/W/28	3	Bachelor's	Sub/Sub	Both–college graduates	All AA
	F/B/58	22	Master's	Urban/Urban	Both–some high school	All AA
2 (2)	F/B/27	3	Bachelor's	Urban/Urban	Mom–some high school; Dad–some college	25 AA; 1 Asian
	M/B/25	1	Bachelor's	Urban/Sub	Both–college graduates	All AA
3 (3)	F/W/61	32	Master's	Rural/Sub	Both–high school graduates	All AA
	F/B/25	1	Bachelor's	Sub/Sub	Mom–some college; Dad–high school GED	All AA
	F/W/45	19	Master's	Sub/Sub	Mom–high school graduate	All AA
	F/W/35	9	Bachelor's	Sub/Sub	Mom–some high school; Dad–high school graduate	All AA
4 (3)	F/W/50	14	Master's	Rural/Sub	Dad–middle school; Mom–some high school	All AA
	F/W/56	20	Bachelor's	Sub/Sub	Dad–unknown; Mom–some high school	All AA
	F/B/46	15	Bachelor's	Urban/Urban	Mom–some high school; Dad–unknown	All AA
5 (3)	M/B/63	36	Master's	Urban/Urban	Dad–military; Mom–middle school	All AA
	F/W/30	3	Bachelor's	Sub/Sub	Mom–unknown; Dad–college graduate	All AA
Music teacher	F/W/61	30	Master's	Rural/Sub	Both (grandparents raised her)–some middle school	
Resource teacher	F/W/66	40	Master's	Sub/Sub	Aunt raised her–high school graduate	
Self-contained special education	F/B/29	5	Bachelor's	Urban/Urban	Mom–high school graduate; Dad–unknown	
Principal	F/B/57	31	Master's	Urban/Urban	Dad–military; Mom–high school graduate	

ANALYZING YOUR DATA

After completing the school and community descriptions, the demographic profile of students, and the survey of teacher characteristics, school leaders and teachers can begin to piece together this information as a way to lead to further understanding of parents and students. (See Figure 1.7 as an example of how a school collected all its information to provide a demographic profile.)

The next step is to analyze the data. For example, in Figure 1.8, Bayman City School is analyzed in a general manner, based on the type of school and general demographics regarding families and teachers. This analysis could become even more useful if done as a collaborative process within a district—as more of a system-wide data analysis—rather than simply school by school or classroom by classroom.

Once you have knowledge about your school type, demographics, and characteristics of families and you recognize your own possible need to think in different ways about parent participation, begin to think of an action plan to involve parents.

In Figure 1.7, Bayman City School is analyzed in a general manner, noting general demographics regarding families and teachers.

Figure 1.7. Example of a School Demographic Profile: Bayman City School

School District: Bayman City School District

School Name: Redmond Elementary School

No. of Students in School: 400

School Type: Urban

Student Demographics (Check for Cultural, Linguistic, and Socioeconomic Diversity): 99% African American; 1% Asian; 100% free or reduced lunch eligibility

Family Description: 65% single-parent families; 11% lived with guardians other than parent (aunt, cousin); 8% lived with grandparent; 6% two-parent household; 10% foster care

Jobs: Entry-level jobs; blue-collar jobs

Education Level: General Educational Development (GED); high school completion; less than high school completion; some college/vocational certification; bachelor's or associate's degree (less than 5%)

Interests/Hobbies: Sewing, dancing, playing cards, watching movies, having cook-outs, attending church, sports, music

Teachers (Backgrounds of School Personnel): 92% White; 8% African American; most raised in a two-parent, middle-class household

Figure 1.8. Sample Analysis of the Urban Bayman City School

What does the information say about the student population?

99% are African American students. All students come from a low socioeconomic background.

What does the information say about the staff population?

7 staff grew up in an urban setting, 8 grew up in a suburban area, and 3 grew up in a rural area. However, 6 teachers live in an urban area, and 12 teachers live in a suburban area; none of the teachers lives in a rural area.

CLOSING COMMENTS

School parental involvement assists in the success of students (Edwards, 2009; Edwards, McMillon, & Turner, 2010; Epstein, 2001). In order to facilitate that involvement, principals and teachers must first learn about the families served by their schools. Conducting a school reality check provides valuable information to assist with the crucial task of reaching out to parents and is well worth the time and effort required. Once you have knowledge about your school type, demographics, and characteristics of families and you recognize the need to think in different ways about parent participation, begin to think of an action plan to involve parents. Chapter 2 provides guidance in devising such a plan.

Plan of Action for Involving Parents

> It takes a village to raise a child is a popular proverb with a clear
> message: the whole community has an essential role to play in
> the growth and development of its young people. In addition to
> the vital role that parents and family members play in a child's
> education, the broader community, too, has a responsibility to
> assure high-quality education for all students.
>
> —National Education Association President Dennis Van Roekel,
> *Parent, Family, Community Involvement in Education*

The changing demographics of our nation provide new challenges for schools seeking to optimize family, community, and school collaboration for the greater good of society as a whole. The first step—gathering information about the community, families, and teachers and analyzing the data—was covered in Chapter 1. With the knowledge you have gained from Chapter 1, school administrators and teachers can use the graphic organizer shown in Figure 2.1 to begin to think of ways to more fully include parents in the school.

ACTION PLAN FOR TEACHERS

The mismatch between teachers' experiences, coupled with the rapidly changing school landscape, indicates that teachers may need assistance in internalizing knowledge related to their school's family demographics.

Examining Social Identity

Having teachers intentionally consider their own background and the background of the students they teach can open their eyes to their

Figure 2.1. Graphic Organizer—Taking Stock of Our School

List the strengths and needs of your school.	List the ways that your school already involves families and communities in school.
Brainstorm ideas (by category, such as technology infrastructure, special needs identified).	Think about the potential strengths of your existing student/family populations that could be leveraged (e.g., guest speakers, volunteers for classroom, bakes sales, connections to community).

own potential biases that need to be addressed in order to become a culturally responsive teacher. The school administrator could ask each teacher to write about his or her experiences growing up: location; school locations and experiences; experiences with parents/guardians; and interactions of school, religion, and occupations. Then ask each teacher to read/reflect on his or her experiences and the similarities and differences of the students he or she teaches. The following resources can help teachers compose their case study:

Cochran-Smith, M. (2003). The multiple meanings of multicultural teacher education: A conceptual framework. *Teacher Education Quarterly, 30*(2), 7–26.

Ladson-Billings, G. (1995). But that's just good teaching! The case for culturally relevant pedagogy. *Theory Into Practice, 34*(3), 159–165.

Raphael, T. E., Florio-Ruane, S., Kehus, M. J., George, M., Hasty, N. L., & Highfield, K. (2001). Thinking for ourselves: Literacy learning in a diverse teacher inquiry network. *The Reading Teacher, 54*(6), 506–607.

Villegas, A., & Lucas, T. (2002). *Educating culturally responsive teachers: A coherent approach.* Albany, NY: State University of New York Press.

The activity of writing a social identity paper can assist teachers in becoming aware of their culture and understanding how it shapes their values, beliefs, and behaviors. This experience can prompt teachers to consider these questions:

- Am I aware of the family strengths and struggles that exist within my classroom?
- How can I connect with parents whose language, culture, and background may be vastly different from my own?
- What can I do to help parents feel welcomed, valued, and positive about the school environment if they may not have felt this way as a student?

Taking a Closer Look at Students and Their Families

If teachers have a large population of students from culturally and linguistically diverse backgrounds, the next step can be to find out about the home countries of parents, family customs and traditions, languages spoken in the home, and other pertinent information. Teachers can accumulate information either from casual parent meetings, surveys, or students. Create a spreadsheet that includes information regarding parents/children and share a wiki with other teachers who may work with those same students (see Li, Sweeney, Protacio, & Ponnan, 2013). A sample is included in Figure 2.2.

Implementing Parent Involvement

The information teachers have gathered about the students and their families helps in considering parent participation and what activities to implement to gain support from parents. Here is a checklist of questions to begin thinking about how teachers can support equal opportunities and diversity for parents:

- How do parents who do not use English as their first language get information about their children's learning and about opportunities to get involved? (This includes parents who are deaf and use American Sign Language, who speak other languages, and who are illiterate.)
- Do teachers and parents have access to translators and equipment that would help them communicate effectively with one another?

- Are parents who have a disability aware of support they can receive to get to the school and to other events, such as Individualized Education Program meetings, teacher conferences, performances?
- Are there opportunities in which parents can bring a family or friend for support to meetings?
- How can parents keep in touch with teachers if they work during the day?
- Is there encouragement and practical help for fathers to be involved?
- Is the school environment welcoming to all parents (fathers as well as mothers)?
- Are there opportunities for loved ones (including foster parents) or partners of parents to get involved as volunteers at the school and be a part of events that celebrate families so that all children will have someone there for/with them?

Teacher–parent partnerships may be new to some staff members who may need support to seamlessly and effectively make this part of their responsibilities. Staff development opportunities may also be needed to support staff members when communicating with parents. For example, workshops for staff on "How to create a welcoming environment for parents" and "Making the most out of parents' time" can help develop ideas and skills. (See also Figure 2.3 for suggestions of activities to involve parents.)

ACTION PLAN FOR DEVELOPING HOME–SCHOOL PARTNERSHIPS

Developing positive relationships with parents is critical to providing the best education possible to their children. Parents are the most important people in children's early lives and are, therefore, the best people to assist school leaders and teachers in getting to know the children. As David Flatley (2009) of Change.org points out,

> Parents are universally accepted as a child's first teacher. It's intuitive, and we usually know it from our own experience. Schools that embrace this reality and recognize the important role parents play in their child's education are better able to create curriculum and build relationships with parents that have a profound effect on a child's journey through school. (p. 1)

Figure 2.2. Sample Class Log with Information

Student	Language(s)	Country or State or City/Town of Origin	Preferred Language of Parent/Caregiver	Refugee (R) or Immigrant (I) or Unknown (U)	Other Pertinent Information
Angela	Spanish [P] English [NP]	Durango, Mexico	Spanish [P] English [SP]		Lives with her parents and four siblings and extended family members; family often travels out of state for seasonal work
Tykesha	English [P]	Baltimore, MD	English [P]		Lives with grandmother and siblings
Sneha	Hindi [P] Urdu [P] English [NP]	New Delhi, India	Hindi [P] Urdu [P]	I	Family lives with relatives
Anna	English [P]	Laurel, MD	English [P]		Lives with mom and three siblings
Chris	English [P]	Laurel, MD	English [P]		Mother ill with terminal disease
Louis	English [P]	Laurel, MD	English [P]		Single mom works two jobs
Shaun	English [P]	Pittsburgh, PA	English [P]		Moved to Maryland; raised by aunt
Rosa	Spanish [P] English [NP]	Juarez, Mexico	Spanish [P] English [NP]	U	Frequently visits Mexico
Alpha	Pular [P] French [P] English [NP]	Guinea	Pular [P] French [P]	I	Living with relatives

Student	Language	Place	Language		Notes
Omar	Arabic [NP] English [NP]	Sudan	Arabic [P] English [NP]	R	Local refugee center assisting with housing
Crystal	English [P]	Laurel, MD	English [P]		Lives with mom, dad, two siblings
Erick	English [P]	Laurel, MD	English [P]		Lives with mom and siblings; mom works night shift
Kerry	English [P]	Laurel, MD	English [P]		Lives with mom and dad; both work during the day.
Letecia	Spanish [P] English [NP]	Juarez, Mexico	Spanish [P] English [NP]		Family returns often to Mexico
Latia	English [P]	Baltimore, MD	English [P]		Mother and two siblings moved to maternal grandmother's home
Brittany	English [P]	Frederick, MD	English [P]		Moved recently from foster care to aunt's home
Javier	Spanish [P] English [SP]	Chihuahua, Mexico	Spanish [P] English [SP]	I	Mother deceased; lives with father and three siblings; travels to Mexico often
Ethan	English	Laurel, MD	English [P]		Lives with parents and two siblings
Alexis	English	Laurel, MD	English [P]		Lives with grandparents

P = Proficient; SP = Somewhat Proficient; NP = Not Proficient

Figure 2.3. Ideas for Parental Involvement

Sport teams	Fundraiser committee: All levels of education
Cooking class	
Home economics	Mediator committee: Parents who are English-as-a-second-language and English speakers
Carpentry: Skilled workers	
Lunch helper/playground assistant: Those parents who are not employed or who are part-time workers	
	Parent resource room/liaison for community: Food pantry, clothing pantry, resources for housing, health care
Chess/checkers	
Mentor for parents/students	Parent council: All levels of education
Classroom helper: All levels of education—they can sign up for once a semester	Parents' evenings committee
	Communication committee
Developing the school library	Pupil focus group committee

Successful home–school partnership depends on the development of mutual trust and respect between school and parents. Schools need to use the skills, knowledge, and experiences that *all* parents and *all* staff bring to the school to support children's learning. The development of good relationships when things are going well can make it much easier for both parents and teachers to make contact with the other when there are concerns. There are many opportunities for *all* parents to have a role in their children's educational success. The checklist in Figure 2.4 can be used by school leaders to assess the current conditions at the school that promote parents' involvement and where improvements need to be made. Subsequent chapters in this book provide further guidance to school leaders seeking to develop effective parent-involvement programs.

ACTION PLAN FOR DEVELOPING
COMMUNITY–SCHOOL PARTNERSHIPS

Schools do not exist in isolation, and school leaders also need an action plan to ensure that there is a partnership between the community and the school. A school is situated in the community it continuously serves. Larger schools may serve more than one particular community; therefore, they need to be aware of any differences in the approaches that are required for each community.

Figure 2.4. Checklist for School Leaders Promoting Home–School Partnerships

1. Is the school welcoming to parents, both in terms of how it looks when parents enter and in the way that the staff greets them?
2. Is there a resource or lounge for parents within the school?
3. Have you solicited ideas from parents?
4. Have you provided opportunities where parents and staff members are able to meet and share ideas as to how all can support the school?
5. Are the activities scheduled at various times so that all parents can be accommodated—weekends, holidays, evenings, and daytime?
6. Are parents informed of and involved in new initiatives? Is there effective communication regarding these initiatives for parents to be able to discuss how they will/can be involved?
7. Are there opportunities for parents to be involved in short- and long-term roles?
8. Are there engaging activities that parents can take part in to get to know all staff and parents outside of the school, such as a barbecue/picnic in the summer?
9. Is information dispersed in ways that will be available to all? Are there any groups of parents, or parents with disabilities or language barriers, who might be excluded?
10. Is there practical support to help parents become involved? For example, on a parents' evening, is there a committee that provides transportation for parents who would not have enough time between the end of their workday and the start of the event to get to the school on time without such transportation assistance? Is there a committee that organizes babysitting service?
11. Has it been made clear that all extended family members are welcome to be involved?
12. Does the school have a way or has it organized a committee to keep track of what specific skills parents have and ways that parents can share their skills and experiences in the school setting?
13. Is there information provided to parents on the requirements needed to help students work within a school setting?
14. Are there other opportunities for parents to volunteer, even if they believe that they do not have skills/experiences to share?
15. Do parents and teachers have a clear understanding regarding the respective roles and responsibilities when parents (and other adults) are there as volunteers and are working with their children as well as other children?
16. Is there a parent liaison to help other parents with resources for adult learning, clothing/food vouchers, tutoring, and so on?
17. Is there easy access to resources for parents who need additional support? Does the school know what additional support is needed?

Schools provide a service that is available for everyone; that makes them a main resource for children and families in the community.

Schools are also part of a network of legal and voluntary organizations that provide services and support to the community. Parents can encourage or build on partnerships between the school and the community. Many schools have already built a solid partnership with those in their community. Figure 2.5 provides a checklist of questions for school leaders as they seek to develop a partnership between the school and the community.

When parents and community members are engaged in the life of the school, the learning environment and the resources available for teaching expand. When teachers and principals build trust with one another and with parents, they can develop a common

Figure 2.5. Checklist for School Leaders Promoting Community–School Partnerships

- Do parents and teachers work together to identify the priorities for the school and identify areas in which help from other people in the community could be useful?
- Has the school identified what particular skills in the community may be useful for the school?
- Has the school identified people in the community who would like to offer their time and skills to help the school?
- Is there encouragement from the school to community members who are not parents of children at the school to become involved? These people could be a part of a child's extended family or have another association with the school. Also, this could be a productive way to invite into the school people who are retired or part-time workers who have more time than parents to provide to the school.
- Have there been opportunities for participation by people who have interests and skills that the students would enjoy? (This is especially important if the school budget does not support special programs such as art, music, and physical education.)
- Have people and organizations been identified who may be able to provide access to different premises? This could be beneficial if buildings are needed to hold meetings or other activities outside of the school.
- Has assistance from local groups been sought in connection with fundraising opportunities for the school?
- Are there events coming up where the school could work with members of the community to increase attendance or promote successful outcomes?

vision for school reform and work together to implement necessary changes in the school. In addition, an intersecting set of relationships among adults (parents, teachers, service providers) can provide a holistic environment in which children are raised with a unified set of expectations and behaviors. Fraatz (1987) uses the phrase "shared sense of purpose" to refer to everyone who is involved in the education of children, whether they work within the structure of a school system or outside of it. Thus, the phrase becomes a kind of link, connecting educators, parents, and community leaders to the cause of educating children and confirming that their authority to do so is a shared responsibility.

The relationship between the school and other community institutions such as businesses and churches can also be understood as a shared responsibility. Interpersonal relationships built between individuals across these institutions provide the glue for innovative collaborations on the institutional level. These partnerships strengthen relationships among people in the entire community, thus building the collective capacity for schools to thrive. Sharing the responsibility for strong schools and for student learning has a direct impact on student achievement (Epstein, 2001; Henderson & Mapp, 2002; see Figure 2.6).

A key element of social change is an ongoing dialogue with community members. Town hall meetings provide an opportunity to communicate with community members and learn their concerns, needs, and questions about care and services in the community for their children. These structured conversations provide host coalitions an opportunity to listen to the community. At town hall meetings, multiple members of a coalition can converse with the audience and ask follow-up questions to clarify responses. Town hall meetings can also serve as a recruitment strategy, motivating community members to join the coalition or become supporters of community initiatives.

Community leaders often have linkages with families that teachers and administrators do not have and can help identify hard-to-reach parents and recruit them, devise alternative solutions to school problems, and help implement these solutions. Without a doubt, community leaders represent a powerful force that can support parents and teachers and help them in achieving their goals for their children's learning and success.

Once community resources have been identified, these resources must be mobilized to help build collaborative partnerships among parents, community organizations, and schools. In order for this to

Figure 2.6. Making the Most of Your Community

Purpose: To identify the resources that are available to support children's learning in the community and to share this information with parents through a community liaison

Step 1: Identify key organizations and community groups.

Organize a directory of all organizations, individuals, and groups that have members in partnership with the school and those who have an interest in becoming a partner with the school. Every committee should produce a list and cross-reference to avoid duplicates.

The list might include the following:

- Children's groups, early childhood groups, after-school clubs (Girl Scouts, Boy Scouts), youth groups
- Sports clubs/activities for children and adults
- Religious and cultural groups and organizations
- Voluntary and community groups
- Key services such as doctors, clinics, libraries, dentists
- Community and adult learning providers
- People who represent the official or formal community such as city council members, police, firefighters

Step 2: Identify those that could help the school, its students, and parents.

Discuss how individuals in those groups and organizations already contribute to the work of the school and how their role might be developed. Identify those who most closely support the mission of the school and who support parents and promote children's leaning and development in the community.

Step 3: Share your findings with parents and pupils.

Invite these groups to a community-welcoming event where they can display information about their organizations. Invite all parents and students and encourage them to attend.

Step 4: Prepare a community directory.

Community groups will be asked to prepare a short paragraph on what they can offer to support children's learning and development. Place these organizations into a community learning directory. Disseminate it to students, parents, and staff.

---

happen, it is imperative for a clear-cut plan, as well as a method of delivery for the plan, to be in place. Individual meetings and also speeches to larger groups will assist with conveying the message of how important it is to build collaborative partnerships between parents and schools early on and with getting community leaders and organizations involved. A confident and well-prepared representative will likely find the best success. (See Resource 2.1, tcpress.com, for a sample speech that might be offered to community leaders and groups; Edwards, 1990, pp. 63–65.)

Parents may, at times, lack the confidence to approach the school, and community partnerships might provide a bridge between schools and parents. Parent councils might act as a liaison between the community and the schools to continuously build partnerships to increase educational outreach services for the school and the community.

REACHING OUT TO PARENTS OF PRESCHOOL CHILDREN

Strong school–community partnerships are especially important when school leaders seek to make early connections with families of preschool children. Then families can begin to build their knowledge of and relationships with principals and teachers before their children come to school. This will enable parents to begin preparing their children for school during the preschool years. Children who have a positive start at home are more likely to feel comfortable, relaxed, and valued, as well as feel good about themselves as learners and have a sense of belonging when they begin school. Ensuring that parents have the knowledge, skills, and resources they need is a step in the right direction.

Over the past 30 years we have recognized the serious gap that exists in educational achievement between the haves and have-nots of society and are increasingly recognizing the early genesis of this gap (Barnett, 2002; Dickinson, McCabe, & Essex, 2006). The challenges low-income families face as they seek to prepare their children for success in school are truly daunting. Our society is slowly beginning to recognize the costs it pays for failing to adequately respond to the needs of such families.

School leaders need to assess the following:

- What preschool education programs are available in your community?
- Has your school district launched such a program in the schools or taken other steps to expand access to prekindergarten programs for local children?

Preschool provides a foundation for learning, both socially and academically, that will help children succeed in elementary school. Study after study suggests that preschool education can have a profound positive impact on a child's development (Gormley, Gayer, Phillips, & Dawson, 2005; Howes et al., 2008).

In a small midwestern community, the public school district opened an early childhood center with a preschool program called the Little Comets Preschool, taught by certified teachers in a convenient community location. The screenshot in Figure 2.7 shows the district's website—providing information about the preschool program and its philosophy. Teachers and parents within the community are excited about the program's curriculum and its connections to the district's educational direction. Students who attend the Little Comets Preschool receive instruction with programs such as Zoo-phonics and Handwriting Without Tears that carry through consistently into the district's kindergarten classrooms. This continuity with early education and intervention leads to student success.

Finding Preschool Parents

Involvement by parents whose children have not yet started school is advantageous for everyone: Early involvement allows a parent a low-stress introduction to the school (Ghezzi, 2014). Ghezzi reveals that she heavily recruits preschool parents by inviting them to school

Figure 2.7. Screenshot of Little Comets Preschool's Website

Little Comets Preschool Program

The Little Comets Preschool Program offers a play-based kindergarten readiness preschool curriculum that teaches intellectual, social and emotional development, language skills, positive self-concepts and self expression through large and small group learning. Preschool children are encouraged to develop independence through daily living and oral language skills through guided and spontaneous interactions. Children explore, experiment and engage in themed activities that are planned for a range of levels in each of the developmental domains.

Early Childhood Philosophy

We believe it is important for children to have learning experiences with peers and caring adults in a fun, positive and safe environment. Early learning opportunities that occur through play-based, child focused programs prepare children to be successful, life-long learners.

events. For example, she suggests the following ways of finding parents and involving them in school early:

- Parents of the 3-and-younger set are easy to find. Seek them out at parks and the pool, as well as churches and local Sunday brunch haunts. Walk over and give them a card with your contact information. Tell them you would love to introduce them to their neighborhood school's parent group. Ask whether they would like some information sent to them.
- Parent–Teacher Organization (PTO) leaders can also arrange to be put on the agenda of open houses at community preschools and also speak at parent co-op preschool meetings to share information about events going on at the school and let people know it is never too soon to join the parent group. It may be worthwhile to consider an inexpensive advertisement in parent co-op newsletters, which parents of young children browse, skim, or scrutinize.
- Some schools host open houses solely for parents whose children are 2 or more years away from kindergarten. Such events give parent group leaders a chance to network with potential volunteers and provide valuable insight to incoming parents. Ask the principal to give an informal talk about all the positive programs going on at the school. Have a teacher discuss the ways parents can get their toddlers and preschoolers ready for kindergarten. Try to include a student performance on the agenda.
- Another strategy is to host events away from the school, such as a movie in the park or a community party. Include contact information on flyers but avoid anything that might be perceived as a hard sell—the goal is to make these parents feel comfortable, not pressured.
- Schools can seek grants or other revenue sources with which to purchase books to give to families with preschoolers to read to young children.
- A tab on the school website can let preschool parents know about events that are open to them. (Ghezzi, 2014)

In addition to these strategies, schools can solicit suggestions from community groups and organizations for finding preschool parents (see Figure 2.8). In addition, schools can provide public service announcements for local radio or TV stations. Also, video or slide

Figure 2.8. Groups and Organizations for Finding Preschool Parents

Social services department	Shelters for abused women
Urban League	Big Brothers/Big Sisters
Interreligious Council and religious leaders	Health department services
	Law enforcement services
Grandparents/aunts/uncles	Sororities and fraternities
YWCA mothers/YMCA fathers	Retired teachers
Housing authority	PTA/PTO members
Director of Adult Basic Education Program	Small-business organizations
	Neighborhood groups/associations
Teen parent programs, such as Parents Too Soon	Local news media
	Public television or cable television networks
Lions Club/Jaycees/Rotary/Kiwanis	
Chamber of Commerce	

program displays and exhibits about preschool can be set up in local businesses, post offices, social services departments, or banks. If the video or slides show local people participating in the program, it will promote more credibility in the community.

In Donaldsonville, Louisiana, where I first piloted the Parents as Partners program, a bus driver surfaced as a key community leader. I also enlisted the owner of a tavern, who drove parents to the weekly sessions and who participated in the program, as well as a Catholic priest who mentioned the benefits of the program as a part of his sermon. My contacts did not include the mayor, the Rotary Club president, or school resource people. They were, however, the natural leaders of the community I was trying to tap.

Small Parent Coaching Groups

The power of peer community and support is profound. A special bond develops among participants of the parent coaching groups based on shared concerns and an understanding of how to help. Small parent coaching groups may provide natural opportunities for helping parents understand how they can support their children's education. For example, enrolling children in preschool and making sure they attend the entire program are important ways to set the stage for their success in elementary school (Barnett, 2002).

You can identify and recruit effective school-partnering parents and invite parents to a parent coaching group to discuss 10 good reasons why children should attend preschool (Broatch, 2014). The 10 reasons are as follows:

1. Preschool is an opportunity for growth
2. Preschool prepares children for kindergarten
3. Preschool promotes social and emotional development
4. The preschool environment is structured, although it may not appear that way
5. Children get to make choices
6. Children learn to take care of themselves and others
7. Preschool promotes language and cognitive skills
8. Preschool teachers nurture a child's curiosity
9. Preschool activities boost pre-math and literacy skills
10. Preschool helps develop motor skills (pp. 1–4)

In addition to encouraging parents to send their children to preschool, parents participating in coaching groups can learn about the importance of getting and staying involved in their children's education, and they can also learn strategies for how to get involved. Parent coaching groups could also be a place where parents learn how to build collaborative partnerships with preschool teachers. Instead of just encouraging parents to send their children to preschool, these coaching groups can begin teaching parents the importance of remaining involved in their child's education rather than just sending their children to a program where they can be educated by other people. Through parent coaching groups, parents can also meet other parents and hear stories of how preschool helped their children to be more successful in school. The parents may also offer ideas for overcoming challenges, such as lack of transportation or lack of knowledge of preschools in the area that are accepting new students.

CLOSING COMMENTS

As the opening quotation of this chapter argued, parents, family members, and the whole community are vital players in children's education. School administrators and teachers can support their involvement by learning about families and community members and devising action plans that include ongoing dialogue with community members, leveraging of existing community resources, and cultivation of new community partnerships that can provide powerful bridges for all parents and family members. Focusing on reaching out to parents during the preschool years is especially important. Finding preschool parents and inviting them to participate in parent coaching groups can help them understand their role in their children's education and be more confident when schools seek to build collaborative relationships with them. To further increase the success of all children, schools need to take action to involve parents, family members, and the whole community.

CHAPTER 3

Engaging in Person-to-Person Interactions with Parents—Make Your Best Opportunities Count

> The school serves as a fertile ground for collaborative efforts among parents, teachers, administrators, community. . . . The school, because of its location and commitment to serve the public's young children, can become the hub of the community's successful collaborative efforts.
>
> —Kay Wright Springate and Dolores A. Stegelin, *Building School and Community Partnerships Through Parent Involvement*

When local schools were closely interwoven with the small communities in which they were situated, as in communities from which some of our ELL students come to us, parents and teachers saw one another at Sunday school, at the grocery store, and at tea parties; we were social networking before it was electronic, and conversations between parents and teachers were ongoing. There was also a barter system: If your child was having a problem in school, you might say to a teacher when you saw them at church, "Is it possible for my son to mow your lawn and then you might help him with his reading?" So, in schools like these, an open house was a celebration, but it was not an isolated opportunity.

As educators, we know that communication between school and home is extremely important to a child's success in school. When school leaders, teachers, and other school staff respect parents and share information with them openly and frequently, parents are more likely to trust and work with the school personnel to support their children's learning. Most of today's schools generally offer three direct interactions with parents: (1) open houses, (2) parent–teacher conferences, and (3) newer, more advanced forms of electronic communication. In

35

this chapter I discuss the first two opportunities for communication. These involve in-person teacher–parent interaction. Chapter 4 looks at how teachers and schools can use 21st-century avenues of electronic communication.

Trust and partnership have a huge impact on not only school and family relationships but also student academic success. Classroom teacher Katie Davis conducted some research to see the correlation between student academic gains and at-home literacy practices where parents were involved in their students' learning. She provided a survey to parents asking for honest feedback on their interaction with the school, homework, and other at-home literacy practices (see the link to the parent survey: docs.google.com/a/glcomets.net/forms/d/12oAI8431CIvHBld5Y46DzXnb9mcXMJh932OR8ZCRUO8/viewform). After comparing survey data from the parents with academic data for the students, she stated the following:

> The data continue to affirm the connection between student learning and at-home literacies and answer my questions about how the two are connected. I currently have four students performing well below benchmark and making little progress. Of these four students, only two of their parents filled out the survey. The data from those parent survey show that both of these students do not often initiate reading at home and do not participate in any recreational reading at home aside from homework. One of the two students does not have a library card, and parents of both students answered that they do not regularly participate in any kind of writing at home either. Both of these students struggle primarily with fluency, although accuracy and retell scores are also below grade-level norms.

Katie's classroom data confirmed her resolve to work with families to support home literacy practices in order to help her low-performing students grow academically.

OPPORTUNITY 1: OPEN HOUSE

The open house continues to be a common event in schools, although teachers have multiple opportunities beyond the open house to connect with parents in order to exchange information that will assist students in their academic and social growth. The purpose of an open house (or back-to-school night) is for parents to have a brief time to be welcomed to the school by the principal, to get acquainted with the teacher (or teachers), to see the classroom, and perhaps to get a quick overview of class expectations and the curriculum for the year. It is not a time for individual conferences, and teachers need to make that clear to parents before the event. It is not an appropriate time for parents to speak to the teacher about their child's specific needs or their concerns. An open house generally begins in the early evening and lasts for between 30 and 90 minutes. This event is usually held right before school begins or the within the first 2 weeks of school. Many times it convenes in a large area such as the gym, where the principal provides information about the school. Figure 3.1 includes topics that a principal might discuss briefly and suggest parents can learn more about through print and website resources. Once the principal has provided a broad vision and shared high expectations for the year, parents have the opportunity to visit classrooms. In other instances, parents only visit classrooms, and the teacher provides all information about the school as well as classroom rules, expectations, and curriculum. In some schools curriculum nights are held for each grade level for each subject throughout the school year. The parents role-play as students, and they are taught the content and provided an opportunity to practice the content. They are asked questions that can help them understand the content well enough to go home and assist their child.

An open house is an opportunity to build connections between family and school, as well as among parents; to let parents know that they are welcome; and to create a larger community of parents, students, and school. A plethora of open house activities exists to engage parents, as described in Figure 3.1 (see also Resource 3.1, tc-press.com; jc-schools.net/ce/OPENHOUSE.ppt; www.vickiblackwell.com/openhouse/Open%20House%20Ideas.pdf).

At an open house an important matter classroom teachers cover is expected classroom behaviors. The Behavior Matrix in Figure 3.2 was developed by a team of teachers at an elementary school in a small midwestern district and is used to teach expected classroom behaviors at the beginning of the year as well as to review them throughout the year. It is shared with parents at the beginning of the year to establish clear expectations and initiate communication

Figure 3.1. Essential Information That Parents Need to Have

All of the information below needs to be shared with parents, in handouts, in a school handbook, and on the school website, and some of it shared verbally at open houses.

1. Rules of the district (e.g., must live within the district to attend school—if not, is there a fee)
2. Rules of the school (behavior plan for the school, for each class, for the district; this document is usually created by district office personnel)
3. Attendance policy
4. Suspension policy
5. Grade change policy
6. Website information/phone numbers/time that school begins and ends
7. The principal and his or her duties
8. Who the support staff are and what support is offered
9. Who the staff members are and what their assignments are
10. How to make contact with the teacher and principal
11. School board meeting dates
12. What is expected of the parent (e.g., serve as a volunteer so many hours a year, attend so many conferences/meetings a year, know what to do to set up a meeting)
13. Whether after-school and before-school programs are available; if so, times and cost
14. What is expected of the student (behavior, volunteer services, homework)
15. Services available to the parent/child (vision and hearing screenings, dental services, testing of students for learning disabilities and other disabilities), where those services are available, and the fee if applicable
16. Regulations for free or reduced-price lunch; applications and when they are due
17. Medical forms that must be filled out and updated

and then reviewed with them as needed based on data analysis of problem behaviors.

Teachers have developed lessons for every area on the Behavior Matrix that all are taught to all students. Figure 3.3 shows a sample lesson. Having consistency in expected school behaviors throughout the school helps assure parents that standards for all students are fair and clear (see also Resources 3.2 and 3.3, tcpress.com).

In sum, the open house becomes the initial introduction between the teacher and students' families. It provides the teacher and parent with opportunities to begin to get to know each other, establish communication, and celebrate the shared purpose of educating children for a bright future in the world. The next event of the school year really brings parents and teachers together in a specific child-centered meeting.

Figure 3.2. Behavior Matrix

	Arrival	Hallway	Cafeteria	Assembly	Bathroom	Playground	Classroom	Dismissal
SAFETY	Use walking feet Report to supervised area Stay clear of bus caution line	Keep hands and feet to self Face forward and stay to the right Walk single file	Wait quietly in food line Walk to and from destination Remain seated while eating	Walk in an orderly manner Sit quietly in rows Keep hands and feet to self	Limit stall occupancy to one person Keep water and soap in the sink Use one squirt of soap	Line up when whistle blows Stay in assigned grade areas Keep hands and feet to self Keep nature on the ground	Use walking feet Keep hands and feet to self Keep desks and chairs on the ground Use materials appropriately	Keep hands and feet to self Leave through correct doors Walk on sidewalks
OWNERSHIP	Neatly put away belongings Go straight to destination Prepare for class	Keep body under control Pick up belongings and clean space Keep voices off	Place lunchbox in class bin Enter at end of line Raise hand and wait for dismissal Clean up all trash before being dismissed Eat your own food	Sit in assigned classroom spots Have appropriate interaction with presenters	Flush Wash and dry hands Keep voices off	Use peace-making process Wear weather-appropriate clothes Include others Throw trash away	Engage in classroom activities Complete work Keep classroom clean Use appropriate voices	Collect all personal belongings Keep backpacks on backs Line up and wait in an orderly manner at bus
ATTITUDE	Be cooperative Be ready to learn	Be friendly Walk with a purpose to your destination Close lockers quietly	Be kind to peers Use *please* and *thank you* Include others Have positive conversations	Clap at appropriate times Cooperate with presenters Be polite	Use bathroom for intended purpose	Play fair and share Be kind and appropriate Have fun Be a good sport	Do your personal best Be an active learner Be kind	Be cooperative Help others Follow directions
RESPECT	Walk on sidewalks Use kind words	Follow adult directions Be kind to others' personal property Use manners Hold doors for others	Use table manners Sit quietly Follow adult directions	Sit on bottom Eyes forward Monitor your own personal space	Give privacy to others Wait your turn	Share playground equipment Play by rules Use playground equipment appropriately	Be considerate of others' ideas Monitor your own personal space Share materials Follow teacher directions	Monitor your own personal space Wait quietly Use kind words

Figure 3.3. Arrival—Lesson 1 (Entering School)

Delta Center Elementary: P815 Lesson Plans
Location for Expectation: Sidewalk and Lobby Area

Safety	Ownership	Attitude	Respect
Use walking feet	Go straight to destination		Walk on sidewalks
Stay clear of bus caution line			
Keep hands and feet to self			
Report to supervised area			

Learning Goal: The students will be able to approach the school appropriately and walk safely into the building. Students will be able to go straight to their supervised destination.

Behaviors Not Allowed	Behavior Expectations
Running	Walk safely into school
Stepping over the bus line	Stay clear of bus caution line
Wandering in the school	Keep hands and feet to self
Touching others	Walk straight to supervised destination

Materials:
None

Provide Opportunities to Practice:
- Model and practice walking safely from the dropoff area into the school
- Model and practice walking safely from the bus line into the school
- Model and practice walking safely to your supervised destination
  - » Lobby bench until 8:25 A.M.
  - » Playground (outdoor recess) or gym (indoor recess) from 8:25 A.M. to 8:45 A.M.
  - » Explain why walking safely is important
  - » Explain why going to your supervised destination is important

Checking for Understanding:
- Ask students, "What does it look like to walk safely into the school?" (Hands and feet to yourself, walking on the sidewalk, taking your turn to get into the building)
- Ask students, "What does it sound like to walk safely into the school?" (Appropriate volume)
- Ask students, "Where do you go when you get to school before 8:25 . . . from 8:25 to 8:45 . . . after 8:45?"
- Ask students, "Where should you go when you get to school at 8:40?" (Join your class outside/gym)
- Ask students, "Where do you go for indoor recess? Where do you go for outdoor recess?"

OPPORTUNITY 2: PARENT–TEACHER CONFERENCES

Traditionally, parent–teacher conferences have been used to provide parents with an update on their child's progress or to discuss difficult situations. Teachers want to exhibit a tactful communication style but not be so polite that they avoid being open and honest with parents. Often these conferences are aligned with the close of grading periods. A more proactive approach is to set up parent–teacher conferences early in the school year as a means for laying the foundation for two-way communication. Take this opportunity to get to know the parent and provide information about yourself, your teaching style, and positive experiences you have had working with their child.

Make Your Messages Respectful

Approach the teacher–parent–child relationship with respect as indicated in the following guidelines:

Be courteous:

- Speak directly to parents using eye contact.
- Use surnames when addressing parents.
- Make statements such as "Thank you for coming," "Thank you for listening," "Thank you for participating," "Thank you for volunteering," and "Thank you for sharing your talent/skill."
- When speaking with the parent/guardian regarding children, be encouraging and make sure that you always list the strengths of the child and then discuss what can be worked on and how.

Be clear:

- Use words that are understandable ("Your child is working at the proficient level, which means she understands at least 80% of all content").
- Provide suggestions that are practical ("In order to help your child with his reading fluency, you need to read to him, then have him to read the same sentences to you").
- State what the issue is and provide suggestions that are achievable ("John's behavior is on yellow—he has to be talked with regarding talking and getting out of his seat without permission on a daily basis; we will do a behavior chart for

him at this desk, and if he gets three out of five green stars in a week, he can earn 5 extra minutes of recess").

- Provide feedback on students' assignments, the grading system, and how you will encourage students to reflect on their own behavior/progress.
- Share where student work will be displayed.
- Outline the procedure as to how homework and notes will be sent home.
- Explain your policy regarding missing assignments.
- State where/when grades will be posted; discuss methods of instruction.

Be helpful:

- Provide resources when applicable (dental, housing, food, homework assistance); provide explicit examples for homework.
- Provide websites that the parent can have the student visit for extra assistance.

Answer General Questions

Parents might ask questions to elicit information and help make their child's year more successful (see below). Teachers might feel that they have addressed many of these questions at the open house meeting with parents but should be prepared to patiently answer these questions and expand upon the information if needed. Frequent questions from parents include the following:

- Could you outline the schedule of a typical day/class period for me?
- What type of *discipline plan* do you use in the classroom?
- What are your *views on homework*, and what is your homework policy?
- What skills are being addressed right now, and how does that tie in to the overall goal for the year?
- Is my child keeping up in class?
- How is my child getting along with other children?
- What *kinds of testing* should I expect my child to participate in this year?

- Does this testing have an impact on my child's academic future or on how my child is graded?
- What can I do at home to reinforce what my child is learning?

For additional questions, see Morin (2014).

Focus on the Child

A great way to start a conference is to have parents read a letter that their child wrote for them. Classroom teacher Katie Davis and her team have students complete a fill-in-the-blank letter for their parents who will be attending conferences (see Figure 3.4). As she begins a conference with each parent, this letter is sitting on the desk to greet parents. It is a positive conversation starter with families and a wonderful self-reflection tool for students. It is important to note that the first contact with parents should be open and positive. This lays the foundation for an open and beneficial collaboration throughout the year.

The conference is an opportunity to show parents a sample of their child's work. Nina Hasty, a former classroom teacher and literacy coach, discovered that during parent–teacher conferences, parents

Figure 3.4. Conversational Starter with Families

Dear _____,

I'm glad you came to conferences! Here are some things you should know!

I think I've really been working hard _____

I am really good at _____

I think I should practice more at _____

I love learning about _____

My favorite part of my classroom is _____

Don't forget to look at _____

Love,

_____

Students fill this page out before parent–teacher conferences, and the paper is waiting for their parents when they arrive. Parents love starting conferences by hearing straight from their own children how they believe they are doing in school.

may need a visual to help them understand the readiness level at which their child functions compared to other students. Figure 3.5 shows examples of students' writing samples that could be used to demonstrate various performance levels and benchmarks or expectations. While the examples shown are for young learners, this practice of sharing examples of work, either from parents' own student or from others, across levels of success is helpful to parents of all students from K–12, just as it is for students.

After presenting the student's work, you can spend a few minutes explaining to parents your professional opinion about their child's work and allow them to make some comments (see Figure 3.6).

Clearly Explain Test Data

While showing student letters to parents and showing examples of student work are great ways to get a conversation flowing between

Figure 3.5. Student Writing Samples

Writing Sample #1

Writing Sample #2

Figure 3.6. Your Professional Opinions About a Child's Work

In Jessica's drawing, she shows understanding of the topic of Antarctica from the details in her illustration. Her picture includes warm clothing, icebergs, and a penguin. The formation of the people in her drawing has many accurate details, and her drawing has a sense of gravity.

In Jessica's writing, she uses a combination of accurate and phonetic spelling. She uses capital letters and spaces between words appropriately. The words written phonetically are easy to recognize. Jessica's writing is above grade level.

During Jessica's conference, I would share her progress with her family. As goals for her continued growth, I would suggest building on sentence complexity, stamina, and instruction in spelling patterns and conventions.

parents and educators, there is also a push right now for more data-driven conferences. In such a conference, teachers review specific data on their child with parents, often compared with national norms for same-age peers. This helps the parents see where their child is performing in terms of academic grade-level expectations. Figure 3.7 provides a sample script of one approach that teachers can take in showing concrete data, explaining what those data indicate to parents who might not have any background or context for understanding the information, and then pointing out specific ways in which they as parents can use the data to influence what they do to help their child with reading at home.

Figure 3.7. Sample Data-Driven Parent–Teacher Conference

Teacher: Johnny is making great progress in 2nd grade so far this year. Let me show you some evidence of what his growth looks like this year. Three times a year he takes a computerized assessment called Northwest Evaluation Association (NWEA) This bar graph [see Figure 3.8; teacher has either printed or projected charts to show parents while discussing the test results] shows you where he scored on the reading portion. The darker bar shows where his score was on his most recent assessment. The next bar displays the district norm (where most of his peers in our district are performing), and the third bar shows the national norm (where most of his same-age peers in our nation are performing). If you look underneath the bar graph, it gives us some more detailed information about his Lexile Range (which is a reading level) and where he scored within the separate areas of literature and foundational skills and vocabulary.

Parent: I see that the bars have gotten higher each time he takes the test. This means he keeps improving, right? But I also notice that he is performing below most students his age in the nation. What can I do to help him get this score up and be a better reader?

Teacher: You are right! He is making progress, and that is so exciting! That means that together as a team, you and I have worked hard to help him become a better reader already! But yes, we want to see him continue to grow. You can take this report home with you. This number here at the bottom shows the Lexile Range for what level books he is reading. We know that students who continue to read a lot of texts at their Lexile level will make gains. If you look on the Scholastic order site, you can actually search for books at this Lexile level. And then when you purchase books or check them out from the library, you can be sure that he is reading the right level! If you'd like, I would be happy to show you how to do that later.

Figure 3.8. Graph of Student's Northwest Evaluation Association Reading Data

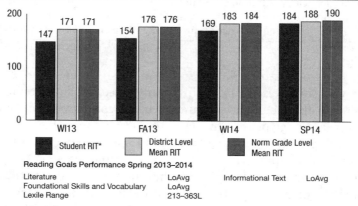

*RIT stands for Rasch Unit. It is a unit of measure that uses individual item difficulty values to estimate student achievement.

In addition to the NWEA data in the example above, teachers can choose to use multiple forms of data to show parents, such as Developmental Reading Assessment (DRA) levels, DIBELS (Dynamic Indicators of Basic Early Literacy Skills), MEAP (Michigan Educational Assessment Program), and so forth. Showing parents graphs and numbers during a parent–teacher conference can help them visually see how their child is doing and where that compares with same-age peers. The important piece of a data-driven conference is to be sure that parents understand the data you are sharing and how they can work with their child.

Summary of Types of Parent–Teacher Conferences

Two common types of parent–teacher conferences are school-mandated conferences and event-centered conferences. School-mandated parent–teacher conferences are usually held once per semester, usually at the end of a grading period. Event-centered parent–teacher conferences may be held at any time, and the teacher or parents ask for the conference in order to discuss a particular issue or pattern of activity. Figures 3.9 through 3.11 at the end of this chapter offer additional information about these two types of conferences.

CLOSING COMMENTS

Open houses and conferences bring families physically into the learning spaces of their children. Face-to-face time offers unique opportunities to establish trust and partnership. When parents do not attend, conferences can be conducted by telephone, emails, or home visits. Telephone calls and emails lack facial expressions and body language and could potentially lead to miscommunication, however. Instead, whenever possible, consider using telephone calls and emails to set up face-to-face interactions with parents. On the surface, this may appear to be creating more work for educators who are overworked already. However, the extra time spent building a positive connection with parents will pay off in the end. Educators will be viewed as partners, not adversaries, when difficult situations arise. In Chapter 4, I discuss a variety of the ways in which teachers can use technology to communicate with parents, which works particularly well once initial connections have been made.

Figure 3.9. School-Mandated and Event-Centered Parent–Teacher Conferences

School-Mandated Parent–Teacher Conferences	Event-Centered Parent–Teacher Conferences
Cultivate a positive relationship with families: Publish conference dates on the school's website in all languages that apply to the parent population. Devote a bulletin board to displaying upcoming conferences and showcasing highlights of previous conferences. Provide translators if possible. Create posters and post them next to each classroom to announce the conferences and encourage parents to sign up for a conference time.	*Student-led conferences (grade 3 and above):* Students select two to three assignments to place in their created portfolio (see Resources 3.4 and 3.5, tcpress.com). They must write why they selected those assignments and what they learned from each assignment. Students create one mini-lesson that they will teach to showcase their knowledge of a subject for their parent(s).
Provide opportunities for parent input during a mandated Parent–Teacher Conference: Have parents fill out a parent-conference form prior to their scheduled conference day/time. The form will provide an opportunity for parents to think about questions that they need to ask and other concerns (see Figure 3.10; Resources 3.6 and 3.7, tcpress.com). Ask parents to share the methods that they utilize at home to assist their child with their homework. Provide parents with an opportunity to review major projects and ask for feedback (questions and comments). Consider scheduling conferences at 20- to 30-minute intervals so that parents can have adequate time to have a meaningful dialogue.	*Focus on behavior:* Students and teachers can reintroduce parents to the rules (and the consequences for breaking those rules) of their class and the school. Teachers can explain to parents their concerns and/or suggestions to continue satisfactory behavior or enter into an agreed-upon plan to assist the student to begin to make better choices. Students who had a difficult time adjusting to the rules and have shown improvement will have the opportunity in conjunction with their teacher to explain the plan of action taken for continuous improvement. The parents will be asked to help with the upcoming plan to continue the progress. Students and parents will interact with one another using topics for discussion that are cocreated by students and the teacher (bullying, how to be and make friends, how to share, how to agree to disagree, being friends with those who have a different background).
Offer specific at-home instructional strategies: Provide brochures with step-by-step examples of problems students sometimes encounter with upcoming curriculum content. See, for examples, Figure 3.11.	*Focus on social:* Etiquette classes among the students, parents, and teacher.

Figure 3.10. Parent Conference Form 1

This form will help parents prepare for a parent–teacher conference prior to the meeting. Parents will have the opportunity to think of and write down questions and concerns to bring up at the conferences.

A conference with _____ [child's] teacher has been scheduled for _____ at _____ in room _____. Please take the time to think about the questions below prior to the conference. You may add questions and bypass any section that is not applicable to you. Please bring this form to the conference with you.

1. What goal(s) do you have for your child this school year?

   _____

2. What specific concerns do you have about your child's academic progress or behavior?

   _____

3. What questions do you have regarding the curriculum, classroom procedures, school procedures, and assessments?

   _____

4. What specific concerns do you have about your child's academic and behavior progress thus far?

   _____

5. Does your child have any concerns regarding school (complete with your child)?

   _____

6. Are there any outside factors that may prevent your child from being successful?

   _____

7. If you have suggestions and any other concerns, please list them here.

   _____

   _____

Figure 3.11. Johnny's Progress: Strengths and Limitations

This is what Nina Hasty observed in her classroom and the strategies that she applied to elevate Johnny's strengths.

Reading	Math	Writing
Comprehension strategies: Retelling, comparing and contrasting, monitoring for understanding	Long division: Creating his own problems	Essays: Using a storyboard on the computer to record his research
Fluency: Reading longer texts and different texts (magazines, newspapers)	Story problems: Using fiction characters in his stories	Recording his story on tape, listening, and then transcribing

These are the limitations that Nina Hasty observed in her classroom. Nina applied the following strategies throughout the next 5 weeks.

Reading	Math	Writing
Nonfiction is challenging for Johnny to comprehend. I will apply think-alouds as I model to show Johnny what he should be thinking of as he reads.	Algebra: I will allow Johnny to write the formulas out on an index card so that he does not have to memorize them; he can perform the steps.	Adding details to Johnny's writing: I will read trade books and allow him to read more trade books so that he can see how the author added details to bring the literary elements to life (setting, characters, and plot).
I will review text features in nonfiction literature.		

This is what Nina Hasty asked the parents to help Johnny with over the next 5 weeks at home.

Reading	Math	Writing
Read at least 30 minutes per night and orally. Three of those nights he should read nonfiction. Ask him to turn the subheadings into questions and answer the questions as he reads.	I will send home the formulas and problems in algebra and have him to do two per night.	Have him take two of the stories that he is reading weekly and add details within the story.

CHAPTER 4

Using Technology to Communicate with Parents

Students are at an advantage when teachers and their parents work together as a team in order for them to do their best at school. Schussler (2003) notes that teacher–parent relationships are considered vital to the development of schools as learning communities. Epstein (2001) describes communicating with parents as one of six major types of parent-involvement practices critical to establishing strong working relationships between teachers and parents. Cultivating communication between home and school helps a teacher know a student better, which in turn assists the teacher in finding the best strategies to meet the needs of the student and thus to teach more effectively.

UNDERSTANDING TYPES OF COMMUNICATION STRATEGIES

In order to build an effective partnership with parents, teachers must understand and employ a variety of communication strategies, in addition to the in-person teacher–parent interactions discussed in Chapter 3. Basically, there are two types of communication strategies: one-way and two-way (Berger, 2000; Edwards, 2004; Hoover-Dempsey & Whitaker, 2010). Newsletters, bulletin boards, report cards, school handbooks, and progress notes are all examples of one-way communication. One-way strategies keep parents informed about activities and school policies. The second type of communication, two-way, is an integral part of building partnerships with parents. It is essential for educators and parents to engage in an exchange of ideas, including exchanging information on assessment and instruction to build productive partnerships (National PTA, 2000). True partnerships with parents can only be achieved when two-way communication strategies are utilized (see Figure 4.1).

Figure 4.1. One- and Two-Way Communication

One-Way Communication	Two-Way Communication
	Parent surveys
Newsletters	Report cards and progress reports that provide a space for parent feedback
Bulletin boards/hallway and classroom displays of student work	Home-to-school communication notebooks (with a space for parents and teachers to communicate through written notes)
Report cards and progress reports	Twitter (this can be used in an interactive way to provide links and information for parents and allow them to "tweet" questions and feedback to you)
Student/school handbooks	
Graded/notated homework and classroom assignments and tests	Classroom Facebook pages (many schools and teachers are using these pages to communicate with families in a way they are familiar with—private pages can be created in order to keep the audience selective)
Text messages (this can be done through a professional, safe mode using the program Remind101)	School and classroom websites and blogs (with interactive areas such as embedded surveys, comment boxes, and Google doc links)
School and classroom websites (noninteractive)	Phone calls
	Emails
Automated phone calls	Pinterest boards

APPLYING TECHNOLOGY TO REACH THE PARENT COMMUNITY

In addition to and within the two types of communication, technology is a great way to keep parents informed in innovative and time-efficient ways. Technology also holds promise for allowing teachers communication opportunities "not limited by school hour or location" (Brewer & Kallick, 1996, p. 181). Ramirez (2001) believes that technology provides educators with the opportunity to communicate quickly to a broad parent community. One example of this is the use of the application Remind101. This app/web-based communication tool allows teachers/schools the ability to send parents text messages through a secure site, without giving away or accessing personal phone numbers. When a teacher sets up a Remind101 account, he or she provides a code to the parents in the classroom. The parents then text that code to a given number (one that is given when signing up for Remind101, not the teacher's personal number). The teacher is then able to send out messages through the app or website to the parent group throughout the year. These messages come right to the parents' phones as a text message, but the parents are not able to see the other numbers included or to text back a response. This is a great way to send reminders to families using a familiar means of communication that many families are comfortable with and access often.

An elementary school teacher from a small midwestern community, Krista Hunsanger, blogs about using Remind101 to connect with families from her classroom (see Figure 4.2). Once parents quickly sign up for free, they are able to receive text messages from her about classroom happenings, homework, and so forth in a safe way without any actual exchange of phone numbers.

American children live in a variety of family forms: For example, while some children live with both parents, many live with only one parent; others live with one biological or adoptive parent and one stepparent. Some do not live with either parent; instead, they are cared for by other relatives or by foster parents or child-care providers. The parents of some children are married, and others are not. Some children live with parents of the same sex. See Figure 4.3 for a list describing members of the parent community who might exist in today's schools.

Figure 4.2. Remind101 Blog

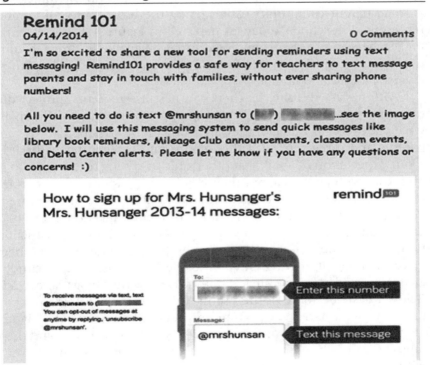

Remind 101
04/14/2014   0 Comments

I'm so excited to share a new tool for sending reminders using text messaging! Remind101 provides a safe way for teachers to text message parents and stay in touch with families, without ever sharing phone numbers!

All you need to do is text @mrshunsan to (███) ███ ████...see the image below. I will use this messaging system to send quick messages like library book reminders, Mileage Club announcements, classroom events, and Delta Center alerts. Please let me know if you have any questions or concerns! :)

How to sign up for Mrs. Hunsanger's
Mrs. Hunsanger 2013-14 messages: remind 101

To receive messages via text, text
@mrshunsan to (███ ███ ████).
You can opt-out of messages at
anytime by replying, 'unsubscribe
@mrshunsan'.

To:
████ ███ ████   Enter this number

Message:
@mrshunsan   Text this message

Figure 4.3. Some Examples of Potential Parent Community Members

Unwed teenage mothers	Foster families
One-parent or two-parent homeless families	Gay and lesbian families
	Two-parent families
Single-parent families	Low-literate parents
Stepfamilies	Culturally diverse parent groups
Working mothers	Unemployed parents
Grandparents	A court-appointed guardian
Unmarried couples	Cousins
Aunts/uncles	An institution employee
Brothers/sisters	Home-schooling families
A group as community surrogate parents	Extended, reconstituted, or blended families
Second-language parents	

Source: Edwards (2009). Reprinted by permission of Scholastic Inc. All rights reserverd.

If family involvement is to become a reality in schools and classrooms rather than simply a professional dream, close attention must be paid to how the family has changed. Similar to Ramirez (2001), I believe that technology enables educators to communicate quickly to a broad parent community. Considering the broad range of families represented in schools today, as depicted in Figure 4.3, it is essential for teachers to use the technological tools available in order to communicate effectively in ways that are relevant and accessible to these diverse parents and families.

With a class website, teachers can post assignments, project due dates, events, and extended learning opportunities and can explain what educational strategies they are using in the classroom, providing parents and caregivers with the opportunity to keep up with classroom expectations. Email is another quick way for teachers to communicate with parents about their child's progress or behavior issues. Newer, more advanced forms of communication are and continue to become available. Often, these forms of communication allow both parents and teachers to communicate without the limitation of school hours or location. These communication tools include, among others, voice mail, email, texting, Skype, Google Hangouts, video technology, school and class websites, PhotoCircle, Twitter, blogs, and wikis. Below I describe some of the useful ways *you* can use these to communicate with parents. One note of caution: Unfortunately, divorce decrees and restraining orders are part of our school reality, and these must be carefully observed so as not to communicate with parents with whom communication is legally blocked.

Voice Mail

Classroom phones permit teachers a flexible opportunity to contact parents from *their* classroom when students are not present. The use of *voice mail* (also known as *voice message*) to augment phone communication has the potential to enhance communication with parents. Over 15 years ago, Clemens-Brower (1997) noted that one creative teacher maintained a daily 1-minute voice mail message for parents and students to call at the end of the day. The recorded messages provided updates on homework assignments and classroom highlights, and also invited parents and children to respond with a message of their own. Perhaps in this day and time, teachers might consider providing voice mail messages recorded in multiple languages. Google Translate as well as a number of other free translation programs can assist with changing the English text to other languages. Keep in mind that even though the translators are useful, they are not always completely accurate in regard to translation meaning. It can be helpful to have a community representative who is available to screen translated messages before they are made publicly available.

Teachers should have a consistent day and time for providing updates to parents. For example, teachers can announce that every Friday by 3:00 P.M. they will record a voice mail message. During the open house meeting, teachers can ask parents for their home/cell number. Teachers can say, "This year we have developed multiple opportunities to communicate with parents—voice mail is one of them. In addition to providing updates on homework assignments, we want to use voice mail for emergency contacts such as school closing alerts, on behalf of a sick child, or other important messages."

Email

Email can be the most efficient and effective way of handling routine matters, such as question-and-answer exchanges between parents and teachers or the scheduling of an in-person meeting. Many schools routinely provide all staff with a school district email address. Teachers should have easy access to a computer to check email at school—and remote access so they can do so at home, too. With access to the email addresses of parents, teachers can daily send a quick list and explanation of all the activities, stories, and notable events from that day. When asked "What did you do in school today?" kindergartners often struggle to communicate—so these daily messages provide specific details parents can use to guide those conversations. Teachers might find composing a quick daily email much less stressful than assembling a newsletter once a week. Email is also a great way to involve parents in signing up for school and classroom activities. Katie Davis, a 2nd-grade teacher, sends an email to parents with a link to a Google doc whenever she needs volunteers and supplies for classroom parties and events. Parents can quickly open the Google doc and sign up for helping out or sending in a snack. This way, parents can see what others have already signed up for, and it saves the time of having to make several phone calls. She often gets many more volunteers when approaching through email because it is such an effective communication avenue for many parents.

A word of caution: Parents who routinely use email for work may expect unrealistically speedy responses from teachers. Avoid parental frustration by clarifying up front that most teachers will be unable to answer email during the regular school day. In most cases, a 24-hour response time is reasonable. And when replying requires an extended or delicate conversation or when a response might be misunderstood, it is best to use email to set up a meeting or phone call.

Texting

Even if parents do not have Internet access, most parents have access to cellphones. Zickuhr (2011) reported that cellphone users are accustomed to receiving informational text messages—for example, banks send text messages when accounts are overdrawn and airlines use text messaging to send flight status updates. Given this foundation, schools and teachers should consider using text messages to communicate because parents are comfortable receiving this form of correspondence. Communicating with parents using cellphones is a unique way to bring parents into the school and into their children's classrooms in real time, particularly for parents who have "smartphones" that allow them to use email, text messages, and the Internet. In addition, smartphones are capable of taking photos and sending these pictures via text messages, email, and the Internet. Schools can begin to communicate with parents using text messaging in several ways at the individual, classroom, and whole-school levels (i.e., emergency communication, event reminders, polls, reaching parents who do not speak English, etc.). However, Stephens (2013) noted the following:

> If teachers agree to expand parental involvement by using text messaging, they may be apprehensive about using their personal cellphones for such purposes. School can provide phones for professional use: the cost of cellular service has declined over the past several years, and it is now possible to obtain group packages that include the mobile devices with unlimited calling and text messaging features. Some packages also include reasonable Internet access rates as well. (p. 2)

Skype

Skype is a software application that allows users to make free video conference calls on the Internet. Since its inception, it has become a popular tool in schools. It is an excellent resource because it allows teachers and students as well as parents to visually interact from the convenience of their own homes.

Schools across the country are beginning to embrace this technology because of its simplicity and effectiveness. All teachers might benefit from learning about Skype and its components, which include (1) a computer, tablet, or phone with broadband Internet access; (2) a webcam (most laptops sold since 2008 include this feature) and a microphone; and (3) a free downloadable version of Skype software.

Teachers can make scheduling parent–teacher conferences easier by using Skype. Teachers can accommodate parents' schedules and still have the opportunity to *show* them what they are doing in the class with Skype as a video partner. (For more information, please see www.behrmanhouse.com/resource_room/9-ways-to-use-skype-in-your-school.)

Google Hangouts

Hangouts bring your conversations to life with photos, emails, and even group video calls. Google+ Hangouts is a free video chat service from Google that enables both one-on-one chats and group chats with up to 10 people at a time. While somewhat similar to Skype, FaceTime, and Facebook Video Chat, Google Hangouts focuses more on "face-to-face-to-face" group interaction as opposed to one-on-one video chats, and it utilizes sophisticated technology to seamlessly switch the focus to the person currently chatting.

Parents need to know that Google Hangouts is a way for kids, families, and teachers to communicate online for free. In the 21st century, where many students come from either single-parent working families or families where both parents must work, coming to school for parents is difficult. Live streaming lets school come to the parent either live or later via recording. Schools can share morning announcements, assemblies, celebrations, and more. Teachers can share student presentations and invite parents to actually join Hangouts at the time their child will be presenting. Student presentations will be there later for parents to share with friends and families to brag about far and wide. Views and comments can also be exciting and motivating for students.

Video Technology

The use of video technology has proven effective as a communication tool with parents. Educators can create a brief 10-minute video to welcome new families to the school including an introduction, a tour of the school, portions of a "lesson in action," and an invitation to become involved in their children's education. This can be especially useful for students and families that move into the school throughout the year and were not able to attend the open house. Providing them with access to this type of video would be a great way to enable them to be informed and feel connected.

Many teachers know how to make spontaneous videos very easily using iPads, cellphones, and video cameras. Impromptu videos can be recorded and shared from phone or tablet. For other videos, such as formal student presentations, you may want higher quality. Even for these, you do not need expensive equipment, but having the right stuff helps. A good camcorder, editing computer, and accessories will improve the quality and ease of *all* your video-making. Using a microphone is essential to create good sound quality. Lighting is key to a great video. Bianca Te Rito (2011) recommends the following steps for developing a video:

1. *Preproduction*—scripting your message, wardrobe, hair and makeup, setting the background

2. *Filming*—lighting, camera positioning, learning your best angles, camera framing and psychology, how to speak and look at the camera, how to overcome distracting mannerisms

3. *Postproduction*—editing, putting it all together. ("How to Choose," 2011)

Later in the school year when you need parent volunteers for clubs and committees such as book club and academic games, tutors, chaperones, committee members, classroom helpers, and so on, you can have staff members work with students to create a 10-minute video that demonstrates and explains each role. These videos can be uploaded to your class or school website. If parents have questions regarding the information within the videos, a question-and-answer section can be created.

School Websites

School websites are the most efficient way to give parents a peek inside the happenings of a classroom or a school. Pictures of school activities, plus calendars, e-newsletters, examples of student work, and week-by-week listings of course assignments and due dates are all just a few of the ways administrators/principals are using the Internet to share important classroom and school information with parents. Remember to allocate enough time in your schedule to keep it current. Alternatively, you can assign someone, or ask the parent council to organize a technology committee and assign the duties to a number of parents who would be able to divide up the responsibilities of updating the website throughout the school year. The parents selected would have to have the time and skills necessary to keep the website current because an out-of-date website is almost worse than no site at all.

And remember this: Never post pictures of students or their full names without written parental permission. Classroom teacher Katie Davis points out that this is a fuzzy area because many schools and classrooms do post pictures with parent permission—including her classroom. She noted that she sends forms at the beginning of the year for parents to notify her if they do not want their child photographed or videotaped. Otherwise, she as well as others in her school use *lots* of pictures on their school and classroom websites—they just do not put student names under photos. Parents love seeing pictures of what is going on at school.

Class Websites

Busy teachers find it hard to take time out of their day to make phone calls or write notes to working parents who may be difficult to contact. A classroom website is an easy and quick way for teachers to keep parents and students up-to-date on what is happening in the classroom. Teachers can put homework, projects, and fieldtrips on the site for parents to see what their children are doing and accomplishing at school. (For sample class websites, see Figure 4.4 and Resource 4.1, tcpress.com.)

Teachers can also put parent-response forms on the site, such as a fieldtrip permission slip or a sign-up for a class event, so that parents have guaranteed, easy access. Send hard copy forms home, too, as not all families have printers.

Teachers should make sure to update the page frequently so parents can rely on it for important information. It is important to offer this information in the home languages spoken by class parents. As

Figure 4.4. Example of a Class Website

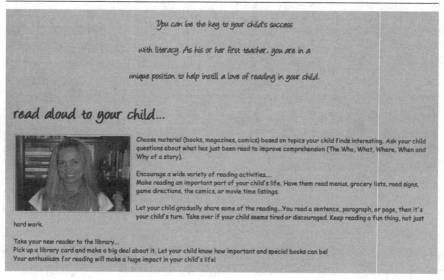

Katie Davis makes it a focus of her class website to provide parents with encouragement and tools for helping their child succeed academically. Teachers can create standard forms for the class website with items regarding academics, behavior, and upcoming events. This form could be a checklist of items that are pertinent for that week or day with a standard paragraph, as shown in Figure 4.5.

Figure 4.5. Examples of Standard Forms for a Class Website

Event example:

> We are going to _____ (fieldtrip name) on _____(date); the amount will be _____. Please place this date on your calendar. I will be sending home a permission slip that you will need to sign and return in order for your child to participate.

Behavior example: Within a website, depending upon the server that the school uses, parents have passwords that they use to access their student's information, and these forms, filled out, would be within the section of "Weekly Progress Report for Behavior." An example for this is below:

> _____ (child's name) displayed the following behaviors (satisfactory, unsatisfactory, respectful to classmates/teachers, not respectful to classmates/teachers, had to be spoken to ___ times during the day regarding talking, uncompleted work, etc.) today.

This can be done by checking off the behaviors with the teacher's initials.

mentioned earlier, Google Translate and other free translation programs can assist with changing the English text to other languages. However, as also noted above, although useful, translations are not always completely accurate in regard to meaning.

PhotoCircle

Because elementary school parents especially love seeing pictures of their children enjoying school, teacher Katie Davis shares pictures with parents through the app PhotoCircle. This is an innovative, cross-platform, real-time photo-sharing app for Android and iOS-powered devices. Initially available only in the iTunes App Store, the app has just made its way onto the Android platform. The purpose of PhotoCircle is simple yet fascinating; for example, as a teacher, you can create a circle (virtual network) in which you can add as many friends (other PhotoCircle users—i.e., parents) as you like, with whom you wish to privately share photos in real time (over Wi-Fi/3G/4G). This means that only parents who are signed up to be in the "Photo Circle" can see the photos. Content sharing across the devices of all the participants is ultra-quick, and you do not even need to manually refresh the photo albums to look for updated content, as it all happens automatically and instantaneously. Each circle is private and accessible by authorized members only.

Twitter

Twitter can open up new worlds to just about anyone involved in education. Family and community reminders and educational resources can be shared quickly and easily through Twitter. An online social networking service and microblogging service, Twitter enables teachers and parents to send and read text-based messages of up to 140 characters, known as tweets. Parents can connect with one another and their children's teachers, students can collaborate or participate in hashtag chats, and teachers can build a robust professional/personal learning network (PLN) (Lepi, 2013). Teachers can tweet with parents about things that they are doing in class, upcoming tests and assignments, school events, and other important activities. (For examples of teacher tweets, see Figure 4.6 and Resource 4.2, tcpress.com.)

Figure 4.6. Screenshot of a Teacher's Twitter Home Page, Featuring Tweets About Classroom Learning, School Events Needing Volunteers, and Upcoming School Fundraisers

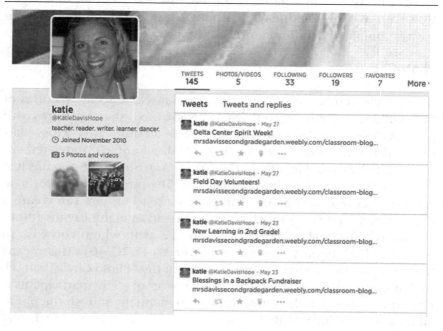

Blogs and Wikis

Blogs and wikis are effective means of communicating electronically with parents. Blogs (short for weblogs) are publicly accessible online journals written by individuals (such as teachers) for others (such as students, families, and other educators) to read and comment on. The simplest way of understanding a blog is that it is an online diary. Teachers and parents can blog about homework questions, fieldtrips, class projects, and so forth. Finally—and perhaps more important— blogs are free. Just a word of caution: Teachers do not want to have the blog turn into a venting forum for unhappy parents. Teachers could address blog and wiki etiquette during an open house in order to set the stage for positive communication throughout the year.

A wiki, from the Hawaiian word meaning "quick" or "rapidly," is a website that teachers, students, and parents can create together by reading and revising one another's ideas and comments. By creating an effective network of wikis, parents, teachers, and students can easily keep up with what is going on in just a few clicks. The school can inform parents about an upcoming standardized test, and teachers can use wikis to share material and facilitate professional development. Teachers can also use wikis to replace their newsletter and stay in touch with parents about what is going on in their class. Wikis, like blogs, allow teachers to embed videos and pictures relatively easily.

CLOSING COMMENTS

From before the first day of school, teachers, parents, and students anticipate what the school year might bring. There is ample opportunity for teachers and parents to engage in productive interactions that might benefit children in their academic and social growth, but it is imperative that teachers make the most of those interactions. Today's technologies can help with the collaborative effort; however, it is important to understand the time and effort that goes into setting up these communications and maintaining them throughout the school year. Once in place, they return the effort not only by saving time but by fostering closer home-to-classroom connections.

CHAPTER 5

Bringing Parents Together Around Things That Matter

> If families are to be involved as true partners in their children's education, it is important to provide ongoing opportunities to hear their concerns and comments as well as providing them information.
>
> —Oliver C. Moles, *Reaching all Families: Creating Family-Friendly Schools*

When children enter school, not only are they affected by the new school environment but their parents are as well (Edwards, 1993b). As Fletcher (1966) reminded us,

> Education is simply not something which is provided either by teachers in schools or by parents and family members in the home. It must be a *continuing* cultivation of the child's experiences in which *both* schools and families jointly take part. (p. 189)

Over 40 years ago Harrington (1971) stated that "schools cannot and would not exist without parents. Parents supply the school with primary material—their children—around which the formal educational and organizational program for that school is constructed" (p. 49). In other words, schools and teachers are here to serve students and families, and an integral part of a teacher's job is relating to parents. Potter (1989) argued as follows:

> Teachers have the important responsibility of working with and relating to families, not just children. Of course, the teacher's role with the child is different from that of the parent. The teacher has a more achievement-oriented approach where performance will be evaluated, but this cannot be done fairly if the teacher has no knowledge of the family relationships of the child. The teacher should strive to develop an

Why does this responsib. rest on the full on the teacher

environment where there is a *participatory role* for the family, which facilitates the parent–teacher–child relationship and so enables the teaching and evaluation of the child to be appropriate and just. (p. 21)

In our mobile world, it is less likely that today's parents and teachers, compared to previous generations, will hold beliefs and values that are closely matched (Keyes, 2002). As pointed out in earlier chapters, when teachers lived in the same communities with school families, there was a "natural bridge" between family and school (Edwards, 2004; Hymes, 1974). Today, teachers often come from a socioeconomic class, race, or ethnic group that is different from that of the children they teach. Differences in these realms are associated with different interactional styles and language systems, as well as values, and present challenges to developing effective partnerships (Burke, 1999; Henry, 1996; Langdon & Novak, 1998). Keyes (2002) correctly noted the following:

> In the last 50 years . . . there have been changes in how schools and families have viewed each other. Because of a developing awareness of the importance of the bridge between home and school, schools have reached out to families and families have pressed to be heard in schools. (p. 181)

Once those connections have been made, it is imperative that teachers take full advantage of the assistance that families might provide. For this particular chapter, I focus on teacher/family/school connections and partnerships to promote literacy. Schools need to bring parents together around important things that matter.

ENHANCING PARENT INVOLVEMENT

Parent Informant Meetings

As the principal investigator of the Home Literacy Project at Kendon Elementary School (a Michigan State University Professional Development School), I created parent informant meetings. A parent informant meeting is a group meeting where teachers and parents collaborate on a grade-level project (see Edwards, 2004). The parent informant meetings established a predictable structure for parents to communicate information about how their child was responding to instruction in school.

Parents not only became more knowledgeable about the school curriculum but also contributed information about their children's struggles, concerns, and progress. They began to inform other parents and teachers about their children's desires, and they made sense of the topics, audiences, and important issues in children's lives. Many parents gave one another ideas about how they wrote with their children and what ideas had stirred their children's curiosity.

Parents became more than recipients and overseers of assignments. Their creative responses also changed the dynamics of the informant group. There was a mutual sense of pride and enjoyment, shared by parents and professional educators alike, in reading the children's writing and explaining life situations and humorous events such as how a garage sale treasure (a plastic fruit–covered hat) became a critical component in a story. They also shared a mutual frustration over students who refused to write or share their work with their classmates. Rather than just expediting the meetings, teachers reaped rewards by openly sharing their struggles as well as hearing from parents about the positive effects of their teaching. For example, one parent publicly praised the work of his child's teacher and described his responses to a relative who criticized the public schools within the district. Other parents described their child's excitement about writing with friends as a sleepover activity. Parents received support from the school and also from other parents.

Parents were truly involved in the group and the group process. The curriculum was not simply handed out and parents were not just told about how their children were learning reading, writing, English grammar, and spelling. The informant meetings, in conjunction with the audiotapes, videotapes, invitations to the classroom, and journals, created an organizational structure for parent interpretation and expression. Parents could listen in on how their child's interests and problems were addressed during in-school writing conferences. More important, the videotaped instruction helped parents visualize and consequently discuss the community of readers and writers that teachers were attempting to build within the classroom. By changing the organizational structure of parent meetings and allocating resources to help parents gain access to information about the school, parents participated in more meaningful ways. They contributed and developed an interpretation of their child's reactions to school assignments, classmates, and their teacher as they developed strong parent–teacher and parent–parent relationships. (See also Resource 5.1, tcpress.com.)

Literacy Network

Many communities throughout the country have a literacy network that schools can partner with. Literacy Network offers its volunteers the chance to apply their skills, broaden their perspectives, and positively change the lives of others. For example, Literacy Network's English in the Schools program in Wisconsin provides adult English-as-a-second-language (ESL) instruction to the parents of children attending schools in the Madison, Verona, Middleton, and Marshall districts. The program helps parents become active partners in their children's education by connecting them to their children's schools. Parents learn about their children's schools and American educational norms while learning English as well as how to improve their children's reading and writing skills. In Ann Arbor, Michigan, throughout the year, Children's Literacy Network participates in special projects, events, and collaborations, such as the following:

- Women, Infants and Children (WIC) Ice Cream Social
- Educational Project for Homeless Youth
- Literacy Coalition of Washtenaw County
- Success by Six
- Reading with children of migrant farm workers
- Packard Health Fair
- Ann Arbor Book Festival

The Detroit Parent Network—Pathways to Literacy (PTL)—is an early childhood parent education program that serves families with children ages 0–5. PTL prepares parents to be their child's first teacher by giving them the tools, skills, and support that they need to ensure their child is ready for school. PTL offers participating families parent education, early literacy coaching, and family support. Specifically, it offers (1) play groups and programs for families; (2) parent workshops and trainings; (3) free books and toys each month; (4) birthday baskets, workshops, and raffles; and (5) a free Detroit Parent Network membership.

Parent Peer Mentoring

In addition to participating in literacy networks for families, it is important for schools to organize parent-to-parent mentoring programs. The role of parents in a child's literacy development is one of the most important things for schools to consider. Some parents benefit from having other parents help them. A parent peer mentoring program can serve as a way to guide and encourage families in supporting the unique learning potential of their children.

Parents are partnered with other parents who will serve as their mentor for that year. In matching partners, try to select a mentor who had a similar challenge to the mentee; this will help the mentee understand that goals are attainable. The mentor can provide an outline of the phases that he or she went through to be successful. The mentor parent can point out the most useful educational resources. The mentor makes sure that the mentee attends meetings and volunteers; monitors that the mentee supports his or her children with homework assignments as well as social issues; and provides transportation to take the mentee and children to the library, museum, and other educational settings. The mentor helps the mentee with how to resolve any issues with staff members; how to ask questions regarding the curriculum; and where to go for assistance with clothing, food, and other outside agencies. Parent mentors can be a key part of school success.

Parent peer mentors sometimes have other titles, such as volunteer mentor, parent mentor, or parent ambassador. Peer mentors are usually parents who volunteer at family resource programs or centers and share their knowledge and experience with others. They help other parents connect with community resources and build support networks. They may also help the program or center find new family participants. In addition, parent peer mentors gain an insider's understanding of the school system and strengthen skills they need to support their own children throughout school. In turn, parent peer mentors become resources and share these skills or knowledge with neighbors, family members, and others. More important, schools can draw on the strengths of families who otherwise might see the school as unfriendly. Schools can become vibrant centers of community as families begin to use them to access adult education classes and multiple services.

LEVELING THE LEARNING FIELD
FOR CHALLENGED STUDENTS

In the 21st century, schools and school leaders have had to grapple with the fact that they are having to address the needs of students some might call "students we worry most about" (Allen, Shockley, &

Michalove, 1995). This group of students includes (1) immigrant populations and (2) students without preparation for school culture. In
the sections below, I discuss the various ways parents can help as well
as how schools and teachers can support these parents.

Parents Can Help Level the Learning Field for Challenged Students

Hold "Information Fairs" about preschool and kindergarten to encourage more children of immigrants to attend preschool and draw
on special education resources, if applicable. This can be done once
a month for about 1–2 hours before/during/after school, depending
on the schedules of the parents. Handouts can be disseminated in the
immigrants' home languages. Consider designating as chairperson(s)
for the sessions immigrant parents who already use these resources
and hold them in a positive light. This will provide those parents who
have not "bought" into those programs with testimonies from "like"
parents, and those parents could also be mentors and/or another resource for those incoming immigrant parents.

Earlier in this chapter, I discussed parent peer mentoring. This
is a great way to work with immigrant populations. Parent support
groups for those parents who have limited educational and/or English
speaking-skills can help eliminate the barriers to accessing support and
resources for their children, especially those who are undocument-
ed. Parent volunteers, along with staff members, can facilitate communication between parents, teachers, and students to ensure that
all parties understand policies, resources, upcoming events, and the
students' and district's roles in the educational system. These groups
or individuals would develop a relationship with community-based
organizations and could offer their services during the Information
Fairs as well as leave brochures in appropriate languages about their
services and contact information for staff. The staff would then be
able to disseminate the brochures and/or contact information to the
parents or include information in newsletters that should go home
biweekly to the parents. The newsletters would keep parents abreast
of the curriculum that is to be taught within the next 2 weeks, homework assignments, upcoming fieldtrips, volunteer opportunities, and
upcoming school events.

After-school activities can build parent–student English and literacy skills. Also, these activities could support the students' cultural

values. Fostering children's literacy is an increasingly common interest of after-school programs serving low-income children. As they work with children day in and day out, after-school providers observe (especially during homework time) that a good number of low-income children are not acquiring solid literacy skills in school.

Many children who have adequate basic skills do not grasp the meaning of what they read, write creatively, or enjoy reading or writing. These perceptions have prompted many after-school providers to wish to do more to foster literacy. Complementing and reinforcing the desires of providers to support literacy development are the interests of parents, policymakers, and funders. Many parents are eager for their children to have time in after-school programs to get a head start on their homework for the next day.

Policymakers and funders, concerned about the academic performance and test scores of children in public schools, also view the after-school hours as available for addressing the issue of children's literacy. Because the need to help children acquire literacy is so pressing, and because the after-school hours are available and open to a variety of creative and enriching uses, it makes sense for after-school programs to focus some time and effort on literacy activity. The question is what a focus on literacy in after-school programs could and should be about. The Southwest Educational Development Laboratory's (SEDL) National Center for Quality Afterschool (2004–2009) developed family literacy events. The goal of family literacy events is to encourage parent and caregiver involvement in the after-school program. Figure 5.1 is a description of the family literacy events after-school program.

Students Without Preparation for School Culture

Schools need to recognize and be sensitive to the fact that many students enter school without preparation for school culture. The following is a list of ways in which a school can help a student, as well as his or her parents, come to understand the school's culture:

1. Provide a student peer mentor for guidance through the structure of the school day.
2. Offer participation in before- and after-school programs to assist with the formalities of the school day, homework, and classwork.
3. Provide counseling (such as with a social worker) to give emotional and educational support—this will help the student express his or her feelings about where assistance is needed.

Figure 5.1. Description of the Family Literacy Events After-School Program of Southwest Regional Laboratory (Austin, Texas)

What Is It?

Family literacy events are special scheduled times when parents and caregivers are invited to visit and participate in activities at their child's after-school program. Events may include workshops on homework or parenting issues; student presentations, musical activities, or plays; or exhibits of student work. Family literacy events may be led by after-school staff, local experts, or community organizations.

What Do I Do?

In order to plan successful events, it is a good practice to invite a group of parents to participate in all stages of the planning process, from sharing ideas to implementation. The families in your own community and school are your best resource for understanding what will entice others to attend. Whenever possible, offer food and child care at your events. It is a welcoming gesture, and on a practical level, it makes it possible for more parents to participate. Look for opportunities to exhibit student work, showcase student talent through presentations, and have parents visit different rooms to meet after-school staff. Aim for a few family literacy events each year to encourage family involvement and familiarity with the after-school program.

Why Does It Work?

At family literacy events, students can practice language and literacy skills when they talk about or demonstrate what they are learning. Parents and caregivers have the opportunity to increase their own skills as they support their children's learning. Participating in a festive, hands-on event can help families feel more comfortable with doing literacy activities at home, a practice shown to improve children's language arts and reading skills. These events can also help after-school staff communicate with parents about their child's reading and writing progress.

ELL Enhancement

There is much evidence that links parental involvement with student success. Yet many parents of ELL students are not fluent enough in English themselves to support their children's literacy development. To address this issue, a number of after-school programs have successfully partnered with organizations that serve adult English language learners. Collaborations like these provide opportunities for adult family members to acquire English language/literacy skills while empowering them to become more involved in their children's education.

When planning family literacy events, include parents and caregivers from different cultural and language backgrounds on your committee. Ask all committee members to serve as liaisons and/or interpreters and encourage them to recruit participants in their communities. Provide promotional materials and invitations in the languages spoken in your community, and expand outreach efforts to include phone calls or in-person contact. It is important to offer transportation and child care for the event whenever possible; a lack of these services can be a major barrier to participation for many families.

4. Investigate whether there is home schooling available to the student for half-days until the student becomes accustomed to the school system.
5. For an ELL, provide a translator or computer software that translates lectures and assignments.
6. Contact the parent liaison in the school to determine whether there is a parent/student who speaks the same language, and partner those families.
7. Give the student a voice in deciding what will be learned and how.
8. Offer hands-on activities, manipulatives, and/or technology (videos).
9. Provide extracurricular opportunities where the student will excel in order to help students promote acceptance and develop self-esteem.
10. For a student with documented special needs, arrange placement in a self-contained special education class, where the student can receive more individualized instruction until the student is able to keep pace in a general education classroom, or in special education for half-days and a general education classroom for the other half-day.
11. Contact the speech pathologist to evaluate the need(s) of the student.
12. Contact parent(s) to determine their needs and offer resources.
13. Attend biweekly or monthly meetings with families to continuously assess their progress and needs.

SHOWING PARENTS WHAT SUCCESS LOOKS LIKE

Schools want parents to be involved in their children's education, and parents want to be involved. All parents want their children to succeed in school. Solid research shows that children from homes where parents are engaged with their children, other parents, and their children's schools earn better grades, get better test scores, enjoy school more, and are more likely to graduate from high school and attend college (Henderson & Mapp, 2002). However, some parents need examples of what success looks like when they work with their children. Often a mentor family can help another family understand that their goals are attainable by describing the phases that led to their own successes.

In parent-led workshops participants can describe what they learned, how that information has been used, and the results. Another strategy is to provide parents with various workshops that will be held at their child's school and the district. These workshops should be geared toward answering questions regarding their child's curriculum and offering strategies that they can utilize at home with their child for greater success (see also Resource 5.2, tcpress.com).

It is especially important for teachers to give parents and other caregivers ideas and tips that will improve their children's potential for success in school. For example, teachers could use video clips to demonstrate to parents how they could help with English Language Arts homework. These video clips could be geared toward seven main comprehension strategies (see Harvey & Goudvis, 2007; Keene & Zimmermann, 2007). Teachers in each grade level could create a mini-lesson as they teach each strategy, making sure that a clear definition of the strategy and modeling were provided. The lesson would consist of questions for parents that they could ask their children. Teachers could supply a list of different books to use with each particular strategy.

A 2nd-grade teacher sent her students' families a survey using Google Forms in order to gain information about at-home literacy practices and literacy materials available to her students when they were at home. The benefit of using Google Forms is that the family responses were organized into a spreadsheet that the teacher could use to plan for supporting families with materials and encouragement to enhance literacy practices occurring at home. Figure 5.2 is an example for the form. This survey provided information about student at-home literacy practices, and the data were used to inform classroom instruction and home support.

As another example, classroom teacher Katie Davis uses blog posts on her class website to teach parents about fluency. She explains steps and tools for parents to use in helping their child with reading fluency—and first understanding what fluency means.

Katie Davis also provides resources for parents and assists them with viewing examples of academic success through technology. She uses the program Raz-Kids, a subscription service, which can be used on iPads by students at school. Students have access to leveled texts that are fluently read aloud to them. This allows students to read the text themselves while recording their own voices. Students may then play back their own voice and listen for appropriate fluency. Some school districts have access to iPads that may be sent home each night, and some students have access to home mobile devices as well as computers and laptops. Parents may sit with their children and listen to the audio of the text first—hearing a good example of appropriate fluency. Parents can then listen to what their children recorded. This allows parents to compare the two and help their children move in the direction of fluent reading because they have a clear example of fluency.

In another blog post, Katie Davis talked to parents about the importance of correct pencil grip. She provided a link to a video that shows them what this looks like and how they can help their child to practice it (see Figure 5.3).

Give Parents Steps to Take and Tools to Use

Neither the school nor classroom teachers can make the assumption that parents know what they mean when they ask them to "get involved." They need to give parents steps to take and tools to use. Below are some suggestions on how to get started (see Resource 5.2, "Reading

Figure 5.2. Survey Information About Student At-Home Literacy Practices

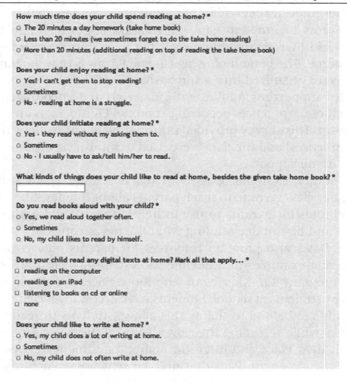

How much time does your child spend reading at home? *
○ The 20 minutes a day homework (take home book)
○ Less than 20 minutes (we sometimes forget to do the take home reading)
○ More than 20 minutes (additional reading on top of reading the take home book)

Does your child enjoy reading at home? *
○ Yes! I can't get them to stop reading!
○ Sometimes
○ No - reading at home is a struggle.

Does your child initiate reading at home? *
○ Yes - they read without my asking them to.
○ Sometimes
○ No - I usually have to ask/tell him/her to read.

What kinds of things does your child like to read at home, besides the given take home book? *
[   ]

Do you read books aloud with your child? *
○ Yes, we read aloud together often.
○ Sometimes
○ No, my child likes to read by himself.

Does your child read any digital texts at home? Mark all that apply... *
□ reading on the computer
□ reading on an iPad
□ listening to books on cd or online
□ none

Does your child like to write at home? *
○ Yes, my child does a lot of writing at home.
○ Sometimes
○ No, my child does not often write at home.

Figure 5.3. Is Your Child Using the Correct Pencil Grip?

Is Your Child Using the Correct Pencil Grip?
10/14/2013   0 Comments

This is an important question for second graders! We are helping your child to work on
handwriting right now - focusing on the correct letter formation. Our district just recently adopted
the Zaner-Bloser handwriting method. One way you can help your child with their handwriting
and letter formation is to start with the basics - check to be sure they are holding their writing
utensil correctly.

Check out this video:
http://www.zaner-bloser.com/media/zb/zaner-bloser/HW_DigRes-1.mp4

- Watch it once by yourself and then check to see if your child holds their pencil correctly.
- Then watch it with your child - helping them grip their pencil the right way.
- Continue monitoring this to help build automaticity with correct pencil grip.

Let me know if you have questions!

Thanks for making a difference in your child's learning!

Strategies That Make Reading Fun," on tcpress.com, which was prepared by Nina Hasty, a former classroom teacher and literacy coach).
A curriculum night could be held more than once a year. A *curriculum night* is an evening, usually held in late September, for parents to
meet the teachers and find out more about the programs offered at the
school. It is sometimes called an *open house* or *meet-the-teacher night*. A
curriculum night could be held for each grade level for each subject
throughout the school year. The parents would role-play as students,
and they would be taught the content and provided with an opportunity to practice the content. They would be asked questions that would
help them understand the content well enough to go home and assist
their child.

Ensure Parents Understand the Benefits for Their Children

Sometimes parents must be shown the benefits—if this is the case,
you can use strategies like having parents show other parents how
their children's papers have improved over time, or having parents
share testimonies of how certain strategies enhanced their children's
learning success. Parents can lead sessions for other parents to help

them understand the benefits of reading to their child, having a quiet homework area, taking their child to the park (outdoors to play) and to the zoo/museum, volunteering, talking with their child about school (e.g., what they learned, what was difficult, any peer issues), scheduling regular doctor visits, attending conferences, and contacting the teacher on a regular basis just to check in.

Your Most Important Messages

Two important messages that teachers should share with parents are the following: (1) the manners required in school and (2) effective parenting for school success. In today's fast-paced, technology-driven society where emails and texts have largely replaced face-to-face interactions and behavior such as texting at the dinner table and in restaurants is increasingly commonplace, teaching children communication manners is something that is more crucial than ever. One of the most important jobs both parents and teachers have is to help children develop social skills, showing them how to interact in a polite manner with people, and to teach them to treat others with respect. These are foundations of academic dialogue and conversation in schools for promotion of learning.

All parents want their children to succeed in school. Thus, it is crucial to give parents and other caregivers ideas and tips that will improve their children's potential for success in school. These ideas also help create a joyful family life and positive connections between *parents and children, parents and parents,* and *parents and their children's schools.* Solid research shows that children from homes where parents are engaged with their children, other parents, and their children's schools (Henderson & Mapp, 2002) show the following characteristics:

- They earn better grades.
- They get better test scores.
- They enjoy school more.
- They are more likely to graduate from high school and attend college.

HOLDING PARENTS ACCOUNTABLE

Parents are the most powerful force on earth. Our laws and policies must take a step toward recognizing that (Epstein, 2001). There are increasing calls for schools to find ways to hold parents accountable for their involvement in their children's education. Porter (2012) provided the following warning:

> Parents who have demanded better teacher quality and heightened scrutiny of schools over the past decade should start by looking in the mirror if they want improved outcomes for their children. Better test scores start at home. And parents may soon find themselves under the microscope for student performance if proponents of parental accountability standards get their way. Although teachers and schools are held accountable for outcomes, many argue that it is time to hold parents responsible, too. The days of parents adopting a hands-off, "it's the teacher's job" approach to their child's education are quickly coming to an end. (p. 1)

Americans are tired of underperforming schools, and they recognize that we cannot continue to blame teachers. Overworked and underpaid educators only see children for a short period of time each day and cannot possibly do everything that a child needs within that time period. How can schools move closer to making parents accountable? Robinson (2011) suggests that the first step is for school districts to distribute report cards showing a student's attendance record, academic performance, conduct, and parental involvement. This would mean a bit more work for educators, to ensure accurate transcripts.

One of the ways in which Nina Hasty, a former classroom teacher and literacy coach, has held parents accountable for communicating is by requiring that they attend a certain number of meetings/conferences—they must volunteer a certain number of hours per month and must serve on at least one (1) committee per year. Committee involvement is paramount. Parents can opt to use technology to be present, if meeting face-to-face is not conducive to their schedule. However, if meeting dates are still not met, parents receive a written letter regarding their nonparticipation. If the parent still cannot attend the meeting(s), they can send a representative on their behalf. This policy would not work everywhere, nor with all parents, but variants are worth considering.

Classroom teacher Katie Davis holds parents accountable for reading to their children. Figure 5.4 is referenced in Katie's classroom blog as well as printed and kept in students' take-home folders. Note the source: the U.S. Department of Education. Not only is it really powerful in displaying parents' responsibility to read with their child every night and encouraging 20 minutes of at-home reading, but it also uses clear data in telling "why." Parents who look at this page should feel a sense of accountability to ensure that their child does not miss out on these reading minutes.

Figure 5.4. Why Can't I Skip My 20 Minutes of Reading Tonight?

LET'S FIGURE IT OUT—MATHEMATICALLY!

Student A reads 20 minutes five nights of every week.

Student B reads only 4 minutes a night . . . or not at all!

Step1: Multiply minutes a night x 5 times each week.

Student A reads 20 minutes x 5 times a week = 100 minutes/week.

Student B reads 4 minutes x 5 times a week = 20 minutes.

Step 2: Multiply minutes a week x 4 weeks each month.

Student A reads 400 minutes a month.

Student B reads 80 minutes a month.

Step 3: Multiply minutes a month x 9 months/school year.

Student A reads 3,600 minutes in a school year.

Student B reads 720 minutes in a school year.

Student A practices reading the equivalent of 10 whole school days a year.

Student B gets the equivalent of only 2 school days of reading practice.

By the end of 6th grade, if Student A and Student B maintain these same reading habits—not counting reading on the weekends or during summer vacation:

Student A will have read the equivalent of 60 whole school days.

Student B will have read the equivalent of only 12 school days.

One would expect the gap of information retained will have widened considerably and so, undoubtedly, will school performance. How do you think Student B will feel about him/herself as a student?

Some questions to ponder:

- Which student would you expect to read better?
- Which student would you expect to know more?
- Which student would you expect to write better?
- Which student would you expect to have a better vocabulary?
- Which student would you expect to be more successful in school . . . and in life?

Source: U.S. Department of Education. (1999). *Start early, finish strong: How to help every child become a reader.* Washington, DC: Author.

CLOSING COMMENTS

At the beginning of this chapter, I referenced a claim that Harrington (1971) made decades ago. She argued that "schools cannot and would not exist without parents" (p. 49). The responsibility for building strong and positive relationships and partnerships with families belongs to schools and teachers. Leveraging families' strengths and supporting their own abilities to practice and develop children's skills outside of school hours can enable schools and families to become partners in children's education.

In order to engage parents fully as partners in their children's education, it is essential for teachers to connect with parents around things that matter and involve parents as peer mentors. This chapter has outlined the most important topics and opportunities for collaborating with parents around curriculum, especially literacy, leveling the learning field for challenged students, and steps toward student success, as well as parent accountability. The specific recommendations in this chapter can help guide teachers and school leaders in intentionally reaching out to parents and creating opportunities to engage them collaboratively as partners who can contribute meaningfully to their children's learning.

CHAPTER 6

Meet Parents Halfway, and Have a Way to Reach Every Parent

As we work with parents, it is especially important that we not forget the complexities of family life. When we see a tired youngster coming to school, we may want to shake the parents and make them read a good article about children's need for sleep. It is easy to forget—or maybe we never knew—that at home three children sleep in one bed while mother and father sleep in the same room with them. We put pressure on parents to come to school meetings as if these were the only true important events of the day. But parents, even very good parents who care deeply for their children, have shopping to do, floors to scrub, hair that must be washed, and often have tired feet and aching backs. You have to avoid the error of seeing life only from the school's side as if homes simply flowed along smoothly with no problems of their own. The closer you move to parents the more realistic your expectations become. Each family has their private story of how it lives its present days.

—James L. Hymes, *Effective Home–School Relations*

The disconnect that many teachers feel with parents who are culturally and linguistically different from them is not as new as we sometimes think. Mrs. Hattie Taylor taught before and after school desegregation. She talked about African American parent involvement in schools prior to *Brown*. Mrs. Taylor's discomfort after desegregation echoes that felt today by White teachers teaching children who are different from them:

> I found myself tiptoeing around the parents, not knowing exactly how to approach the White parents. I did not know if they wanted my opinion or if they would respect it. The hands-off approach seemed safe to me and other teachers. (Edwards, 1993a, p. 353)

PLEAS FOR HOME–SCHOOL COLLABORATION

Mrs. Taylor was not alone. After school desegregation, researchers began to plead for educators to develop a closer working relationship with the home. Fletcher (1966) was quick to build the case: "Education is simply not something which is provided either by teachers in schools or by parents and family members in the home. It must be a *continuing* cultivation of the child's experiences in which *both* schools and families jointly take part" (p. 189). Potter (1989) continued this line of thought by candidly stating that "teachers have the important responsibility of working with and relating to families, not just children" (p. 21). Seeley (1985) makes the following argument: "The crucial issue in successful learning is not home or school—teacher or student—but the relationship between them. Learning takes place where there is a productive learning relationship" (p. 11). In Gordon's (1979) plea to educators to develop a closer working relationship with the home, he stated the following:

> Parent involvement holds the greatest promise for meeting the needs of the child—it can be a reality rather than a professional dream. Of course, the bottom line is not only that involving parents holds the most realistic hope for individual children but also it serves as a hope for renewing the public's faith in education. This faith is needed if public schools are to continue as a strong institution in our democratic form of government, which, ironically, can only survive with a strong educational program. (pp. 2–3)

Berger (1991) recognized both the profundity and the modern difficulty of family connection: "The school and home . . . have a natural opportunity to work together" (p. 118). However, it should be noted that the opportunity to collaborate may not seem very natural to teachers today who may not live in the communities where they work, may speak a different language and represent different cultural backgrounds, and may not have many natural, everyday encounters with parents.

RECOGNIZING PARENT DIFFERENCES

In thinking about parent involvement and developing family–school partnerships, educators must understand that parents are not all the same. Parents are people, too, with their own strengths and weaknesses, complexities, problems, and questions, and we must work with them and see them as more than "just parents." In my work with parents, I coined two terms, *differentiated parenting* and *parentally appropriate*, to help teachers find new ways to think about whom parents are. *Differentiated parenting* means recognizing that parents are different from one another in their perspectives, beliefs, and abilities to negotiate school. While parents might have the same goals for their children (i.e., to read, write, and spell; to think well to solve mathematical and other problems; to gain a foundation in history and science; and to develop their intellectual strengths), they might have different ideas about how they can help their children accomplish these goals (see Edwards, 2004, 2009; Resource 6.1, tcpress.com). *Parentally appropriate* means that because parents are different, tasks and activities must be compatible with their capabilities. For example, parents who do not read well might be very intimidated and frustrated by teachers who expect them to read to their children every night, and teachers might need to select other activities to support them in developing reading fluency (see Edwards, 2004, 2009). Parents who work multiple jobs or who are raising their children by themselves might not be able to attend parent conferences after school or in the early evenings, and teachers might need to make other arrangements to accommodate them.

When we as teachers plan activities and tasks designed to engage parents in collaborating with us and supporting their child's learning, we must remember that most parents will want to successfully accomplish them. We as teachers should work to provide as much support as possible to assist parents in completing these activities and tasks.

Case of Lack of Understanding

When we as teachers ask parents to "read to their child," more times than not we assume that parents know what we mean. Unfortunately, many parents do not. I found this to be true in my study of the book-reading practices of poor and minority parents at Donaldsonville Elementary School (see Edwards, 1992). The following anecdote illustrates my point:

> Donaldsonville Elementary School had been recognized for its "good curriculum," even though teachers were disappointed with the progress of their students. Eighty percent of the student population was

African-American children, and 20% was white children; most were members of low-income families. Teachers felt that they were doing all they could to help these children at school. Without parental assistance at home, the children at Donaldsonville were going to fail. The teachers' solution was to expect and demand that parents be involved in their children's education by reading to them at home.

The teachers felt that this was not an unreasonable request. There is good evidence of positive gains made by "disadvantaged" elementary students when parents and children work together at home on homework and learning packets. What the teachers did not take into account was that 40% of the school's parents were illiterate or semi-literate. When the parents didn't seem willing to do as the teachers asked, teachers mistook parents' unfamiliarity with the task being asked of them, coupled with low literacy skills, for lack of interest in their children's education. The continued demand that parents read to their children at home, which had a particular meaning in teachers' minds, sparked hostility and racial tensions between teachers and parents. Each group blamed the other for the children's failures; each felt victimized by the interactions. Children were caught between their two most important teachers—their classroom teacher and their parent. (Edwards & Young, 1992, p. 76)

To further illustrate this point, I share with you the thoughts of one mother and the response of a 1st-grade teacher. Angela, a 32-year-old African American mother with five children ranging in age from 22 months to 16 years old, becomes fearful and sometimes defensive when her child's teacher requests that she read to her child. The mother quietly admitted to me something that mirrors the reality of some parents:

I'm embarrassed, scared, angry, and feel completely helpless because I can't read. I do care 'bout my children and I want them to do well in school. Why don't them teachers believe me when I say I want the best for my children? I know that my children ain't done well in kindergarten and first grade and had to repeat them grades. My older children are in the lowest sections, in Chapter 1, and are struggling in their subjects. My children are frustrated, and I am frustrated, too. I don't know how to help them especially when the teacher wants me to read to them. These teachers think that reading to children is so easy and simple, but it is very difficult if you don't know how to read. (Edwards, 1995, p. 54)

Mrs. Colvin, a 1st-grade teacher at Donaldsonville Elementary School, expressed her frustration with parents or other caregivers like Angela:

> Year in and year out these parents who are mostly low-income African American and white send their children to school with serious literacy problems. It seems as if the children have no chance of passing. They don't recognize letters of the alphabet, numbers, and they can't even recognize the letters in their own name. Consequently, it is not surprising that most of them have had to repeat kindergarten and first grade. All of the kindergarten and first grade teachers have seen similar behaviors in these children. These behaviors include limited language skills and the inability to interact with adults. We feel that these children have not been read to and have rarely engaged in adult–child conversations. Each year when we see parents at the beginning of the school year we tell them the same old thing, "Please read to your child at least two to three times per week. It will make a world of difference in how well your child does in school." We know the parents hear what we are saying, but we don't think they have read or plan to read one single book to their children. We, as kindergarten and first grade teachers, cannot solve all of these children's literacy problems by ourselves. The parents must help us. (Edwards, 1995, p. 55)

Categories of Parent Differences

Jenkins (1969) challenged schools by posing this question: "[Schools] are accustomed to making the concept of individual differences in the children central to much of [their] planning and thinking, but do [schools] also apply [the concept] to [their] contacts with parents of the children?" (p. 35). Making her case even stronger, Jenkins categorized five differences in parents, which pointed to the complexity and significance of schools and teachers knowing the parents they serve or being "parentally appropriate." These five categories are as follows:

- *Parental dynamics.* Teachers have been trained to understand child differences. We try to be patient with a child who cannot learn as quickly as some others and offer extra help to the youngster whose background is inadequate. We may recognize that a child has an emotional problem and try to work with him or her in as supportive a fashion as possible. But we do not consider parental differences. We are more likely to think of parents and even plan for them as a group labeled "parents." "So when . . . [our efforts to involve parents fail to] recognize that parents are different, we may find ourselves frequently distressed or disappointed at the failure of these parent involvement efforts" (p. 35).

- *Parent feelings regarding school.* Parents respond to schools based upon their past experiences, or frozen memories, in addition to the current situation. Most parents form ideas about what goes on in school from their own school experiences. If these experiences were unpleasant, parents might not feel comfortable returning when their children are in school. However, parents can also be very involved in their children's schooling, based upon their positive school experiences or even the wish that their parents had been more involved in their school experiences. This complex issue of parents' frozen memories in school will be discussed further in the next section.

- *Parent relationships with their children.* Today's parents have different relationships with their children. Some parents relate to their children as friends. Other parent figures, such as grandparents who are raising their grandchildren, might have a totally different way of relating. Even though parents may love their children, some parents are better at relationships than others. Some are warm and supportive; others may be rejecting or even negligent. Some we judge to be highly intelligent, competent people, while we may judge others to be mentally inadequate, unable to grasp the meaning of situations involving their children. Teachers' assumptions about parents are not always accurate and may reflect a lack of understanding of the home culture and language/literacy practices.

- *Parent values and goals.* Values differ among parents. The goals and standards for their individual families will differ one from another and indeed may be quite different from our own. Also, parents value education differently. Jenkins (1969) notes that "some have a high regard for education, but there will be others who view schooling as something to be lived through because it is required by law" (p. 35).

- *Parent attitudes toward involvement with the school.* The school has a responsibility to acknowledge and accept that parents bring their individuality to parent-involvement efforts. Until the school knows parents as individuals and is sensitive to and willing to accept their individuality, it will be difficult to establish any clear communication with them.

Jenkins's (1969) description of the categories of parent/families differences provides insights into the importance of gaining a deeper knowledge of understanding the "human side" of families. If educators begin to think seriously about Jenkins's categorized five differences of parent/families when planning family involvement initiatives, it will move them closer to implementing my notion of *differentiated parenting* and *parentally appropriate*. Also, it will enable educators to develop more inclusive and sensitive practices of family involvement.

Parents' Feelings About School

Jenkins's categories of parent differences are closely connected to how parents interact with their children at home and to their general perceptions and attitudes toward school. However, Berger (1991) expands on Jenkins's category of parent feelings regarding school. She points out that parents respond to schools based upon their past experiences as well as the current situation. Berger characterizes parent responses to school as follows:

> Debilitating experiences with schools, feelings of inadequacy, poor achievement by children, and pressures of the present can cause some parents to stay away from the school. On the other hand, some parents tend to dominate and to be compulsively involved with the schools. Between these two extremes are parents who need encouragement to come to school, parents who readily respond when invited, and parents who are comfortable about coming to school and enjoy some involvement in the educational process [see Figure 6.1]. Each group requires a different response from the professional staff. (p. 118)

Potter (1989) also focuses on parent responses to school in terms of parents' past memories about schools and the feeling that they have nothing to contribute. He argues that

> participation . . . will vary in quality depending on the attributes of the child, parent, and teacher as well as on the social stresses placed on the family and school alike. Parents sometimes feel uneasy in the school environment and this may be simply a hangover from unhappy days at school

AVERY®

**Name Badge
Badge**

Do not apply to leather, suede, velvet,
corduroy, silk, vinyl, or plastic.

Ne pas appliquer sur le cuir, le suède,
le velours, le velours côtelé, la soie,
le vinyle ou le plastique.

▼
Peel Here
Pelez Ici

Figure 6.1. Parents Respond to School

| Parents who avoid school like the plague | Parents who need encouragement to come to school | Parents who readily respond when invited to school | Parents who are comfortable and enjoy involvement in school | Parents who enjoy power and are overly active |

for them; they may feel threatened by the teacher, unsure of "new approaches" in schools or feelings of failure. . . . It may explain why the parents are never home when the teacher makes the scheduled home visit.

Sometimes the parents do not see themselves as educators and do not recognize the important role they have in supplying experiences to the child, which enrich his life. . . . Perhaps the parents feel that teaching and learning all happens at school . . . that they have nothing to contribute. . . . Perhaps the parent has too many personal problems and simply is unable to cope with something else in their lives. In fact, the parents may be crying out for support. (p. 22)

Berger's and Potter's descriptions of parent responses depict the realistic ways in which families react to being invited to come in to school. Parental differences are real, and this is an issue that teachers in the new millennium must seriously consider and appropriately address. Failure to acknowledge and respect parental differences will more than likely result in strained relationships between the home and school. Educators can no longer expect successful family involvement without strongly considering and responding to the human side of families.

LEARNING ABOUT CULTURAL ISSUES INVOLVING
FAMILIES AND COMMUNITIES

Viewing families from a humanistic stance is important, but there is one other approach that educators must consider—the cultural approach. The cultural approach focuses specifically upon the needs of diverse families and emphasizes the fact that families' cultural differences should not be viewed as deficits. Berger (1995) revealed the following:

> Two challenges face the schools as they work with culturally diverse students. One is to understand each child's abilities and actions. The other is to eliminate ethnic discrimination. The more the school and home become involved with each other in a positive relationship, the greater are the opportunities for understanding the family and reducing discrimination. (p. 105)

In addition, today's educators should not make damaging and inaccurate judgments that parents who comprise new family structures are uncaring, incompetent, or apathetic (Compton-Lilly, 2009; McLaughlin & Shields, 1987). Educators should not assume that successful partnerships cannot be developed when certain families do not respond to the school's invitation to participate. Even though today's teachers may not fully understand the possible differences that exist between themselves and observed families, they cannot simply conclude that these "differences" translate into defects in families. As a preservice or experienced teacher, you can work not only to adeptly interpret these dissimilarities or discontinuities but to find successful ways of helping your students deal with them. The differences can actually enhance the educational process.

We must keep in mind that children do not learn in a vacuum; they bring their culture, family experiences, and community experiences with them to school. It is apparent that when people talk about diversity, it always tends to come back to where children come from. At an early age, children become literate as they interact with family to meet personal needs, gain self-identity, and establish behavior patterns that reflect cultural values and beliefs (Heath, 1989; Schiefflin & Cochran-Smith, 1984; Wertsch, 1991). Berliner (1986) correctly noted the following:

Teachers have no choice but to inquire into each student's unique culture and learning history, to determine what instructional materials might best be used, and to determine when a student's cultural and life experiences are compatible, or potentially incompatible, with instruction. To do less is to build emotional blocks to communication in an already complicated instructional situation. (p. 29)

The involvement of families in schools moves closer to becoming a reality when teachers understand more about the cultures of families. Many teachers may be well intentioned and sensitive to different cultures. However, they may lack the experiences and knowledge to understand and meaningfully teach diverse students and to successfully interact with families. Connecting home and school literacies can be difficult for teachers because it requires a deeper understanding of the lives, histories, and cultures of families and communities that may be different from their own.

In teaching in the 21st century, there is an overwhelming need for teachers to understand the culture of students and families. Irvine (1992) correctly points out that teachers must understand the cultures of their students because culture is "the sum total ways of living that are shared by members of a population," consisting of "rites, rituals, legends, myths, artifacts, symbols, language, ceremonies, history, and sense-making that guide and shape behavior" (p. 83). Culture is what children bring to school; John Ogbu (1995) referred to this process as students bringing into the classroom "their communities' cultural models or understandings of social realities and the educational strategies that they, their families, and their communities use or do not use in seeking education" (p. 583). According to Diamond and Moore (1995), "the child's culture, home, family and community form the sociocultural backdrop for school learning. The classroom must be sensitive to these multiple histories, which are the ways of knowing and learning that students bring" (p. 18).

In the new millennium, it is critical for educators to reexamine their classrooms to determine whether they, as teachers, are cognizant of the multiple histories and ways of knowing that students bring to the learning environment. Teachers with students from up to 30 different cultures cannot know all of these cultures deeply but can learn from students and families and show respect for all cultures.

Children's Funds of Knowledge

In an important article Lisa Delpit (1988) critiqued aspects of progressive pedagogy. She claimed that those children who do not learn particular conventions of literacy at home have difficulty acquiring them at school. In many ways this section on culture is an exploration, and I hope a further formulation, of the tension Delpit identified—the tension between honoring the child's home discourse or way of communicating as a rich source of knowledge and learning itself and yet wishing to put that discourse into meaningful contact with school-based and discipline-based ways of talking, acting, and knowing. When teachers do not respect what children bring to school, that has direct implications on family involvement. When families feel that teachers are not successfully working with their children, it oftentimes hampers their involvement in the school.

In her book on *Culture in School Learning*, Etta Hollins (1996) describes several successful interventions that improve the academic achievement of groups traditionally underserved in the nation's public schools. Common characteristics of these programs include the following:

1. Legitimizing the knowledge the children bring to school.
2. Making meaningful connections between school learning and cultural knowledge or knowledge acquired outside of school.
3. Creating a hybrid culture in school that is congruent with many of the practices and values children bring from the home and peer culture.
4. Creating a community of learners where collaboration is the norm rather than competition.
5. Balancing the rights of students and teachers.
6. Providing curriculum content and pedagogical practices that support a consistent and coherent core of identity and intergenerational continuity with the past. (p. 14)

In critically examining what Hollins (1996) has suggested, teachers and school leaders need to look at their schools structures or teaching practices to determine which of the six characteristics of successful interventions have been addressed, which have not, and what additional information might be helpful. In particular, you might start by asking how teachers can begin to celebrate and respect students' diversity. Traditionally, some teachers think of addressing cultural diversity as what Derman-Sparks and Edwards (2010) refer to as a "tourist curriculum," which focuses on artifacts of other countries, such as food, traditional clothing, folktales, and household items. Derman-Sparks and Edwards criticize the "tourist curriculum":

> Tourist curriculum, a superficial educational approach, does not make diversity a routine part of the ongoing, daily learning environment and experiences. Instead it is curriculum that "drops in" on strange, exotic people to see their holidays and taste their food, and then returns to the "real" world of "regular" life. That "regular" daily learning environment is shaped by the cultural norms, rules of behavior, images, and teaching and learning styles of the dominant U.S. groups (middle-class, White, suburban, able-bodied). (p. 8)

So, how do teachers move from seeing culture as "tourism" to seeing it as an important part of our experiences and lives? One way is for teachers to understand how various cultures may foster specific interactive styles that differ from the teacher's expectations. Christine Bennett (1999) believes that culturally relevant teachers seek "intercultural competence"—the knowledge and understanding of their students' cultural styles." Bennett further explains that these teachers

> feel comfortable and at ease with their students. Intercultural competent teachers are aware of the diversity within racial, cultural, and socioeconomic groups, they know that culture is ever changing, and they are aware of the dangers of stereotyping. At the same time, they know that if they ignore their students' cultural attributes they are likely to be guided by their own cultural lenses, unaware of how their culturally-conditioned expectations and assumptions might cause learning difficulties for some children and youth. (p. 38)

Hollins (1996) points out that

> as a classroom teacher, you bring your own cultural norms into your professional practice. The extent to which your teaching behavior will become an extension of your own culture exclusively or will incorporate the cultures of the students you teach may be influenced by your perceptions of the relationship between culture and school practices, political beliefs, and conceptualization of school learning. (pp. 2–3)

As teachers, then, you must seriously examine the relationship between your own cultural beliefs and practices and those of your students. Your role as teacher ought not and should not provide legitimacy to your values and discourse practices at the expense of those of your students. Specifically, you should consider the ways in which accomplished teachers are able to weave together their own cultural patterns with those of their students.

In the 2003 synthesis *Diversity: School, Family and Community Connections*, Boethel recommends that schools engage in many of the strategies already discussed here to address student and family needs related to diversity. In a 2005 SEDL report, Ferguson summarized Boethel's strategies, which I have further summarized below in Figure 6.2 with space for teachers and leaders to add their own plans as shown in Number 6.

Schools or teachers may want to use these strategies one at a time, as a series, or as an idea bank for planning parent collaboration that is more contextualized to a specific location. Using these strategies as opposed to more traditional strategies—such as sending home written notices and asking parents to meet with you at school and on your timetable—will involve taking extra steps to connect with and involve parents in ways that are welcoming, supportive, and responsive to their unique characteristics and situations. Yet it is these extra steps that may make the difference in meaningfully engaging parents in collaborating with schools to support students' learning.

Figure 6.2. Strategies to Address Student and Family Needs

1. **Welcome family members to the school.**
2. **Meet on their turf.**
3. **Remember once is not enough.**
4. **Make use of all communication channels.**
5. **Promote a wide spectrum of involvement. Avoid reliance on a select group of volunteers**. (Sometimes, when one parent or one group is given too much authority or responsibility, other parents are shut off.)
6. **Take time to talk to parents about what they believe.** (One of the common assumptions in education is that everyone has the same beliefs or understandings about student learning. This is actually seldom true.)

Meet with family members and talk about key classroom issues such as student learning and classroom expectations. These sessions can be formal or informal.

Engage family members in an activity that explores the values that parents express about their children's future.

Get Parents Comfortable Talking

Communication is essential to collaboration, as I emphasized in Chapters 3 and 4, and most schools and teachers know that good communication with parents is an important part of their job. Teachers need to know about the children's families, language, and culture in order to help children learn. Parents benefit because they learn more about what goes on in school and can encourage learning at home. Most important, children benefit by improved communication because contact between home and school helps children learn and succeed.

But parent–teacher communication can also be hard, especially when parents feel uncomfortable in school, do not speak English well, or come from different cultural backgrounds than teachers (Kreider, Mayer, & Vaughan, 1999). In Figure 6.3 is a list of strategies for getting parents comfortable talking, which are drawn from my own work with parents and teachers. These suggestions can open the lines of communication between schools and parents by making parents feel accepted, supported, and welcomed as partners in their children's school learning.

Collaboration Among Diverse Groups

Many culturally diverse students and families find it very intimidating to participate in school activities. Therefore, it is important for educators to create a bridge between home and school by creating opportunities for parents to understand that they are a very valuable asset to their child's learning. In an effort to celebrate and cultivate an environment that celebrates and values the families of the ESL program at a small midwestern elementary school, ESL teacher Carmela Rademacher developed a project that celebrated her students' home cultures, diverse experiences, and families, at a level deeper than tourism that also developed student writing and other skills. Parents were asked to send in pictures of their families, foods that they eat, traditional clothing, travels, celebrations, and religious practices. Students were involved in creating books about their families by writing multiple drafts through the writing process. Once each student's writing sample was ready for publishing, the students created ebooks, which were printed for the celebration. They also created posters that showcased their pictures, invitations for parents, and a prerecorded introduction of themselves to be viewed during the book celebration.

Figure 6.3. Strategies to Get Parents Comfortable Talking

- Pair parents up with other parents who have similar needs.
- Ask parents for suggestions for book titles for certain topics you will cover, videos to use as a supplemental resource for a topics you will cover, and topics they would like for the teacher to incorporate (with administrator approval) during the school year.
- Provide a suggestion/comment box where both anonymous and nonanonymous suggestions/comments can be made.
- For parents who may stutter when speaking in public, arrange for them to upload a voice recording or type out their information and have their child or another adult read their suggestions/comments aloud.
- For parents who may not be able to use their voice, have them write down their thoughts or have a phone system set up for deaf/hearing loss.
- For parents who are blind or have loss of sight, make braille literature available and have audio messages sent to their phone so that they are able to communicate.
- For parents who do not speak English, identify a translator and/or use online translation tools.
- Make efforts to contact each child's parents throughout the year using their preferred forms of communication. Include positive comments about a child's work, behavior, or personality, as well as any concerns you may have. This will help parents to not be on the defensive and to become more relaxed, which will help them feel comfortable speaking with the teacher regarding any issues they or their child may be experiencing.
- Explain the American school system to parents who may have grown up under the school system of another country. Help them understand that parent involvement can have positive effects on their child's ability to succeed in school. Explain that you wish to support the child's cultural heritage, not replace it. Extend opportunities for parents to share information about their home language and literacy practices so you can try to integrate them into the classroom. This may help the parent feel at ease and be more willing to open up the lines of communication.
- Let parents know that your classroom is a safe haven and that nothing discussed will leave the area—make them feel comfortable disclosing any information that will help you to help them and their child as well as help them to better partner with you in helping their child.

During the day of the celebration, students stood by their books and posters as classmates and teachers visited the book celebration (see Figure 6.4). Students practiced their oral language skills as they eagerly shared information about their families and cultures. There were many meaningful conversations between the ESL students and their classmates. Many students read their books to their classmates. Parents were invited to the celebration at the end of the day. They were asked to bring desserts from their countries. Parents came in, and the children shared their books and posters with their parents. The teacher reported that there was standing room only after the parents arrived.

Figure 6.4. A Cultural Writing Celebration for Students and Their Families from Different Countries and Cultural Backgrounds

Student writers stand near their posters and books they have written, as other students browse the displays, read about their different cultures, and ask questions about the pictures they see. Some students have flags and other artifacts on the table that represent their family's cultural heritage.

ESL teacher Carmela Rademacher looks on as her students present their written works about themselves and their families.

Students have created books that include color pictures of their families and important information about their cultures. Some captions tell about traditional attire and authentic ethnic foods that are present in their homes.

Videos of the students telling more about their cultures play during the celebration.

The success of this project was twofold. First, the project was geared toward a personal celebration. It was not just a superficial recognition of students' customs and cultures; it was about their families. It also gave the parents the opportunity to participate in this project in a nonthreatening way by having them send in the pictures. Second, the students were so excited to show their parents what they had accomplished, as were parents to see what their children had created with the pictures and books. This year-long project generated enthusiasm as it went along.

Assignments and events such as this one bring home cultures and literacy practices into the school in a friendly and inclusive celebration that values each student and his or her family. This can demonstrate to parents that collaboration between people of diverse cultural and linguistic backgrounds is not only possible but also valuable.

REACHING OUT TO PARENTS WITH SPECIAL CIRCUMSTANCES

Unemployed Parents

In the report *Unemployment from a Child's Perspective* (Isaacs, 2013), the Urban Institute and First Focus note that while children could benefit from having more time with their parents at home, parents who lose their jobs can be irritable, depressed, and may shift from parenting that is supportive to parenting that is punitive.

About 6.2 million children lived in families with unemployed parents in 2012, and that number rises to 12.1 million American children—about one in six—when including families with unemployed or underemployed parents during an average month of 2012. This latter figure represents a decrease from 2010, when the figure was about 13.5 million children, but a huge increase from 2007, when the number was 7.1 million children.

These children may especially feel the effects of their parents' unemployment in their education:

> One of the earliest signs that children are not doing well is their school performance. Several studies have documented lower math scores, poorer school attendance, and a higher risk of grade repetition or even suspension or expulsion among children whose parents have lost their jobs. . . . [P]arental job loss increases the chances a child will be held back in school by nearly 1 percentage point a year, or 15 percent. (Shah, 2013, p. 1)

If educators build collaborative relationships with parents, they can be more aware of when families may be experiencing difficulties such as unemployment and can work proactively to engage parents and support students through these times. For example, a teacher may offer an unemployed parent a fixed volunteer role to give the parent a sense of purpose and importance, which he or she may lack during a time of unemployment. This would also help strengthen the relationship and collaboration between the teacher and the parent. Knowing what is happening in the lives of students outside of school through communication with parents and community members is a necessary prerequisite for involving and supporting family members when they face unemployment and other challenging circumstances.

Parents Who Speak Other Languages

All parents can be helpful in their children's literacy development, regardless of their language, education, or literacy level. Parents who speak little or no English can contribute to their children's education in valuable ways. Here are some ways to build an ongoing relationship with parents by reaching out through their native language (Colorín Colorado, 2007); see also Chapter 3.

- *Find a fully bilingual interpreter.* Schools can provide interpreters and cultural advocates for parents who speak little English and/or come from other cultures. Whether a school employee, parent liaison, family member, friend, or community member, this person can translate for parent–teacher conferences, back-to-school nights, PTA meetings, and regular communication. It is best to find an adult and not rely on the student as the translator, as this practice can disempower the parent.
- *Translate the written communications that you send home.* Find a way to send home personal notes and materials in multiple languages. This will keep parents in the loop on issues such as report cards, school events, and homework. Try to offer complete translations in a straightforward manner that parents can understand. You can also translate information verbally into a recording/video link on the school's website.
- *Learn some of the language yourself.* Even if it is just some common words and greetings, using the parents' language will make them feel welcome. Teachers and parents can use translation software whereby they type text in their spoken

language and have the program translate it into the other person's language.

- *Put parents in touch with bilingual staff.* Give parents a list of names and phone numbers of bilingual staff in the school and district whom they can contact to deal with educational concerns. Also encourage them to reach out to other parents who are bilingual or monolingual so they can share experiences and help one another.

Taking these extra steps demonstrates to parents that teachers value their input and collaboration because they are willing to make the effort to communicate in ways that are accessible and meaningful to the family regardless of the language or culture they represent.

Young Parents

Becoming a parent, at any age, can be a life-altering experience. Regardless of race, education, and socioeconomic status, motherhood—and fatherhood—uniformly places demands on one's life that were nonexistent prior to the birth of a child. When school-age students become parents, the new responsibilities can be overwhelming. For teenage parents who lack support from their own parents, this experience can be even more daunting as they seek support in adult-oriented systems, which even older parents may find challenging.

Teenage parents—or students with children, as they are also referred to in the literature—are parents between the ages of 13 and 19. Often, these students drop out of school because of the pressures they experience, including stigmatization associated with early parenting; isolation from peers; and lack of needed support from family, friends, schools, social service agencies, and other organizations (Kost, Henshaw, & Carlin, 2010).

Teenage Parent Programs (TAPs) are located in different regions around the country. The programs enable pregnant and parenting teens to continue their high school education and become responsible, competent parents. A strong academic program adds appropriate electives to the mandated subjects. These electives cater to the students' special needs and support their efforts to become independent, self-sufficient young adults with confidence in their ability to succeed and to help their children succeed, too.

TAPs can occur at the home school, or a student can enroll at a center. At the home school, skilled teachers will work with the teen parents in a group before or after school, 1 day each week for an hour. High school students can earn credits for these courses.

Support services built into the program emphasize counseling, comprehensive health education, practical living skills, an understanding of child development, and peer support. An on-site nursery provides child care during the school day and gives the teenage mothers the opportunity to learn hands-on parenting skills under the supervision of registered nurses while completing their graduation requirements.

Incarcerated Parents

The nation's growing prison and jail population has raised serious questions about the collateral effects of incarceration on children, families, and communities. Whatever one's views about the appropriate role of incarceration in the criminal justice system, it is clear that imprisonment disrupts positive, nurturing relationships between many parents—particularly mothers—and their children (Christian, 2009). In addition, many families suffer economic strain and instability when a parent is imprisoned. Research suggests that intervening in the lives of incarcerated parents and their children to preserve and strengthen positive family connections can promote healthy child development. Schools can work with incarcerated families in the following ways:

- Supply parents with information about what their child is learning.
- Provide access to records: grades, absences, behavioral issues, certificates, results of tests for visual/dental/hearing/learning disabilities.
- Enable web chat so that the parents can read with or to their child or their child can read to them.
- Facilitate email communication.
- Skype during school performances or put performances on a school's website (with a school media release form from parents of children performing).
- Try to enable incarcerated parents to call the school and speak with the teacher/administrator/social worker regarding their child.

- If children can write, have them compose letters to their parent who is incarcerated (with the custodial parent's permission).
- Encourage teachers to read age-appropriate books regarding the topic in their classroom.

Classroom teacher Katie Davis describes how she worked with an incarcerated mother:

A couple of years ago, I had a student in my classroom whose mother was in prison. I actually met her at the beginning of the year—as she requested a meeting with me. She was very open in talking with me about some mistakes she had made and about how she would soon be serving a two-year sentence that her family was aware of and trying to prepare for. She talked about her wishes for her child, shared with me communication tips for working with her husband and mother, and asked if I would be willing to communicate with her through email. She was a loving mother who had made some mistakes and was trying to do everything she could to get things in order for her child before she left. Although, I believe that this is probably similar to many parents who have served time—while they may not all have the gift of time and freedom to prepare before serving their sentence. In late fall, she left for prison and it was a very difficult time for her son in my classroom. He needed a lot of extra hugs, kindness, and understanding. He often met with our school counselor, who had been meeting with him before [his mother] left to help him prepare. On weekends that the family would drive many hours to visit her, he would return to school tired and without homework done. He was facing a struggle that the other students were not. And while I still had high expectations for him, he required some extra support to help him meet his needs. I would often give him the option of catching up on reading and homework during recess if he wanted help from me. I also borrowed some children's books from the counselor about grief, being away from a family member, and dealing with a parent being incarcerated. He was allowed to read these books during independent reading time, rather than simply choosing from the classroom library. This helped him stay focused when it was sometimes hard for him to do. He was also allowed to write letters to her during writer's workshop and I kept a little station with stamps, envelopes, and her address in a convenient spot for him. Surprisingly, her facility allowed her occasional access to the Internet, and we corresponded through email about his academic and emotional growth throughout the year. She was also able to see our classroom website, with updates about what was going on in our classroom, which she appreciated because she had this information to talk with him about when he came to visit. I also had to be sensitive to his situation when referring to a silly word work routine that I had always used. I used to have a section on my word wall labeled "jail." This is where we put the words that did not follow conventional phonetic rules. During most years, this was a fun way for the students to remember these words. But in being sensitive to this family's situation, I removed this section of our word wall. This year was a challenge for this young student. But with the teamwork of the family, teacher, and counselor, we helped him to be much more successful than any of us would have been able to do on our own.

This example demonstrates that by tailoring collaborative efforts to a family's unique circumstances, teachers and school leaders can overcome the obstacles that too often stand in the way of home–school collaboration and of students' success.

Parents Who Are Illiterate, Semiliterate, or Functionally Illiterate

As the number of illiterate adults continues to grow, increasing numbers of children have parents with limited reading and writing skills (Edwards, 1995; Farris & Denner, 1991). Such children are deprived of the joys of reading, for their parents do not read to them. Leichter (1984) observed that "it may be that children can learn to become literate on their own without formal instruction, but when experiences with literacy take place in family environments, the emotional reactions of the parents can affect the child's progress significantly" (p. 46).

If the nation's goal is to break the cycle of illiteracy, teachers need to aid illiterate parents in building the desire to read and write in their children by providing them with the tools of literacy. Teacher–parent interactions should be characterized by sensitivity, understanding, and responsiveness to the parent's needs. Some suggestions from Nina Hasty and colleagues for working with illiterate parents to increase these parents' role in their children's learning can be found in Figure 6.5.

Figure 6.5. Strategies for Involving Illiterate Parents

- Schedule parent–teacher meetings, if at all possible, around the parent's schedule and offer childcare.
- Encourage the parent to orally share stories about their childhood or stories passed down from their relatives with their children—the parent is helped to understand that storytelling is a literate practice that is part of many cultures and helps their child with oral-language development.
- Encourage parents to read simple children's literature to their children (nursery rhymes, preschool books, picture books). This provides the parent with a sense of self-esteem that they can contribute valuable lessons to their child even if they are not the best reader.
- Provide visual aids for the parents instead of a list of literature to take to the library. These visual aids require little reading, such as photocopies of the covers of picture books, wordless books, and/or predictable books to retrieve from the library or a store.
- When speaking with parents, always speak using a vocabulary that they will understand. When discussing their child's academics, have examples of their work and examples of the academic level their child should be working on or working toward.
- Link parents with resources within their community that could provide tutoring for them, and see if the parent is willing to be tutored by a high school or college student (free of charge—check for citizenship programs where students have to provide a required number of hours of community service).
- Make home visitations. Since many parents may be uncomfortable even coming to the school out of fear, teachers can do home visits. Within these visits, the teacher can model reading behaviors that will help the parent help the child as well as him- or herself. Example: Parents can be encouraged to use wordless picture books so that the parent can tell the child a story and vice versa. The teacher can demonstrate matching beginning and ending sounds of words with pictures, or matching simple pictures with words underneath the picture so that the child and parent can identify the correct word with the picture. Also puppets can be used to help the parent/child become storytellers.
- Encourage parents to listen to books on tape with their child as they follow the literature.
- Have children's videos that originated from literature available for parents to borrow: *Charlotte's Web*, *Whistle for Willie*.
- Encourage parents to discuss current topics/events with their children at home.
- Hold workshops for parents at the school (as often as there is a need and volunteers) to help parents with their reading skills.
- Recruit other parents who had similar issues and have made progress to be mentors for those parents who are struggling with being illiterate, semiliterate, or functionally illiterate.

Recognizing the unique situation of each parent who may have low levels of reading and writing ability enables teachers to engage these parents as partners in a way that fosters the parents' own learning as well as children's learning.

Parents of Children with Learning Disabilities

All students benefit from family engagement in their education, but children with disabilities often require a greater degree of parental involvement and advocacy than their peers without disabilities in order to be assured of receiving the same level of instruction as the general student population (Ferrel, 2012). Children with disabilities often face multifaceted classroom challenges requiring special attention from teachers and active engagement from their families. Their families play a number of supporting roles, including serving as their advocates and providing valuable insight into their specific needs to teachers, who may at times feel pressed by trying to meet the needs of groups of students. There are rarely any simple answers to balancing the needs of each individual child with disabilities with others' needs, and competing structural, bureaucratic, pedagogical, and emotional factors often add extra layers of effort and complexity for everyone involved. However, when families and educators work together as partners, it enhances the likelihood that children with disabilities will have positive and successful learning experiences. Some suggestions for working with parents of children with learning disabilities are listed below:

- Establish an alliance in the building with teachers, support staff, parents, and child (who have to understand the process, accept the diagnosis, and plan the next steps for the child's future).
- Provide resources that will help parents help their child such as books, the opportunity to check out a computer if they do not have access to one in their home, and a parent hotline for questions about homework and/or projects.
- Engage parents in planning instruction, interventions, and other supports for children's learning and progress in school, being especially attentive to cultural issues and home literacy practices that can be leveraged to maximize student learning and success.

These approaches can help engage the parents of children with disabilities in more meaningfully supporting their children's learning in collaboration with the school.

WORKING WITH SOCIAL SERVICES

School social workers, through their unique training and practice, provide a variety of professional services that foster students' physical, social, emotional, and academic growth. They promote and support the educational process by meeting the individual needs of students and families within the community. These services include providing crisis intervention and counseling, strengthening and supporting parent and family involvement, planning and developing school-based interventions with educators, engaging community resources, and assessing the need for special services. School social workers are often involved in helping students and their families with learning, behavior, and/or attendance concerns while strengthening home, school, and community partnerships.

School social workers may serve early childhood through adult education in all of a district's elementary, middle, and high schools on an itinerant basis. Social workers can be leaders in several programs, which include attendance remediation and dropout prevention, bilingual teams, alternative education, homeless services, kinship care, migrant services, and mental health counseling for identified students.

Classroom teacher Katie Davis describes her relationship with social services:

> Over the years, I have had many students whose families work closely with Community Mental Health and have caseworkers assigned to them from the social work office. If the parent consents, I am able, as their teacher, to communicate with their social worker, counselor, and caseworkers about the students' growth. This has been so important—in order for them to share with me concerns about things they see at home as well as the ability for me to share with them concerns I may have about their academic, social, and emotional growth at school. We are also able to communicate with each other about successes and strategies that have helped the students. This saved us time in figuring out ways to help the child. It can also be arranged for students to receive outside counseling support from Community Mental Health during school hours. In extreme cases, where this counseling would really benefit the students, and when parents are not able or willing to get them to the counseling outside of school, we have arranged for this to happen. Even though they may be meeting with the counselor during instructional time,

we have to prioritize meeting the students' basic needs before reaching them on an instructional level. Without frequent communication between the school and the agency, this kind of teamwork and accommodation would not be possible.

In addition to working with social services, some schools bring in *community advocates*. Katie Davis works with a number of community advocates at her school:

- Community social workers/counselors
- Junior Achievement
- DARE program—local law enforcement lessons
- Community volunteers
- Dog Reading Program—Katie has a volunteer who comes in to read with kids with her service/therapy dog. He is trained to snuggle up with the students calmly, listen to them read, and make them feel happy and safe. This provides excellent opportunities for students who need this positive interaction with others.

Reaching out to social workers and community advocates opens a network of resources for teachers themselves and for parents as part of the collaborative partnerships teachers are working to foster between home and school.

CLOSING COMMENTS

In summary, it is essential that teachers and school leaders recognize that every family is unique and that different families benefit from and respond to different ways of connecting, communicating, and collaborating. When teachers invest the extra time needed to make initial connections with families in ways that are welcoming and accepting of each individual family's circumstances, culture, and language and literacy practices, they will begin building relationships that can open the doors to greater communication and collaboration between home and school. Because children identify so strongly with their families, if you make family members feel welcome, you're making their children feel welcome. Approach the teacher–parent–child relationship with respect. Treat this relationship the way you would treat any really important one in your life.

CHAPTER 7

Overcome the Ghosts in the School and Its Community

First impressions of a setting are a decisive factor for parents. A positive response to their initial inquiry regarding the setting is the foundation to the partnership. All members of staff have a shared responsibility to ensure that the [families] are made to feel welcome.

—London Borough of Havering, *Working in Partnership with Parents*

For most of my school years I attended segregated schools. There I observed that African American parents had a sense of value and pride because the African American principals and teachers made them feel needed, wanted, and included in the business of the school (Edwards, 2004). I vividly remember as a young child how River Road Elementary School was viewed as an inviting place.

During the last 2 years of high school, I was moved to a desegregated school. Although the quality of education for African American children might have improved in desegregated schools, African American parents seemed to have been left out of their children's educational lives. What my parents and I noticed most strikingly in my desegregated high school setting was that we were not included in PTA meetings as we had been in segregated school settings. My parents often reminisced about how the principals and teachers in segregated school contexts made parent involvement a top priority. What was missing but sorely needed in my desegregated high school setting was an invitation for African American parents to be involved in the business of the school (Edwards, 2004).

RECOGNIZE GHOSTS IN THE SCHOOL BUILDING

Morton Professional Development School (a pseudonym), where I had the privilege of coordinating the Home Literacy Project in 1990, experienced a transition similar to the one that took place in my own community in the 1960s as a result of desegregation. In 1952, when Morton was built, it served primarily middle-class White families. These families were young first-time homeowners. The school for them served many purposes. Many of the community's social events were held at school. The school was also a place where the young families discussed national, state, and local politics; goals and aspirations for their children; and ways they could help the school better serve the needs of their children. An interview with the first Morton PTA president was quite revealing. In it, she said,

> In 1952 because there were few obvious differences between parents and children and teachers and administrators, Morton was a place where parents and teachers worked closely together. We were able to work closely together because we were friends, neighbors, church members, and we even saw each other at the local grocery store. We shared so much in common. We had a shared sense of goals and aspirations for our children.

An interview with Mrs. Holmes, a teacher, who had taught at Morton for more than 35 years, illustrates a crucial point in the ebb of parent relations at Morton and marks an important transition between the shared community of the early Morton Elementary School and the Morton of later development. Her comments raise an interesting set of issues that impact Morton even today. Mrs. Holmes reported the following:

> In 1965, when schools were desegregated, "the people in charge" never prepared us teachers to teach minority students, nor did they have sensitivity sessions to discuss our fears, doubts, or opinions. If you tried to ask questions back then or appeared to be against desegregation, you were immediately labeled a racist. In other words, no one seemed to care about how we as teachers felt. The only apparent goal of those in charge was to physically bring together Black and White bodies under one roof. At the beginning of desegregation, we teachers were so caught in our own perceptions of desegregation that we did not even stop to think about how the Black parents felt. In retrospect, I would say if those in charge informed Black parents the same way they informed us, I can predict these

parents probably had the same fears and doubts we as teachers had. When Black children entered Morton, we [the teachers and administrator] saw a sharp decline in the number of events held at school. In the past, the school had been the center for community activities. Many teachers did not want to come back to school at night. It might sound stupid and crazy, but it was very real back then. Parent involvement as we had known it earlier simply did not exist.

The accounts by the PTA president and the Morton teacher, as well as my earlier account of parent involvement in a segregated setting, revealed two forms of parent involvement—one based on a shared sense of goals and aspirations and another based on discontinuity. The teachers I met at Morton in 1990 appeared unaware of the school's history and attempted to interface with parents as if no previous history existed. This failure to recognize the school's history retained in the memory of the community proved problematic for both teachers and the school's administrator until I explained how *ghosts* exist in schools. These ghosts are invisible. No one can see them, but they do exist. Over the years, parent memories of these friendly and unfriendly ghosts signal to parents whether to feel invited or uninvited to come into school. My contention has been supported by Epstein (1988). She warned that schools should investigate their previous histories because "schools of the same type serve different populations, have different histories of involving parents, and have teachers and administrators with different philosophies, training, and skills for involving parents" (p. 58). Understanding the baggage that comes with the institutions will help teachers and administrators build and rebuild a foundation for effective communication.

The failure of schools to build or rebuild linkages between home and schools inadvertently encourages parents to maintain their frozen memories or their community's frozen perceptions of what that school was once like. This perpetuates the frustrations of teachers when parents say negatively, "Things will never change." Such a comment from a parent sounds simple and easily dismissible, but it may convey a very complex and intricate perception. The statement may sound like a personal complaint, but teachers must acknowledge the possible history behind it. In order to unpack such claims, we need to begin thinking more carefully about parent involvement and moving it beyond high rhetoric to high practice.

DON'T BLAME FAMILIES—BUILD TRUST

Just as ghosts in the school building may affect families' involvement in schools, other barriers and obstacles to family involvement may exist. As tempting as it may be to blame families for their lack of involvement, building trust by examining and addressing these barriers and obstacles is more likely to lead to higher levels of family involvement. We can begin moving from rhetoric to practice by examining home, community, and school relationships in today's schools in order to determine the next steps from where we are now. Even though many schools struggle to actively engage high numbers of family members in children's schooling, of those families who do get involved, the majority are White and middle income, typically those whose home culture most closely matches the norms, values, and cultural assumptions that are reflected in the school. Minority families, lower-income families, and families who speak limited English, on the other hand, are often highly underrepresented in school-level decisionmaking and in family involvement activities—a phenomenon that speaks far more often to differing needs, values, and levels of trust than it does to families' lack of interest or unwillingness to get involved (Antunez, 2000; Goddard, Tschannen-Moran, & Hoy, 2001; Trumbull, Rothstein-Fisch, Greenfield, & Quiroz, 2001).

A common misperception about families who are not actively involved at school is that they simply "don't care about their children's education" (Mapp, 2003, p. 42). Educators who see the same small group of families helping out in the classroom, attending school events, and participating in school governance, for example, may conclude that the others in the district are not interested or do not place a high value on education. In fact, as I have pointed out earlier, most families do care a great deal about their children's education. Although White, higher-income families tend to be more visible in many schools, the vast majority—in all ethnic, linguistic, and socioeconomic groups—support their children's learning at home in a variety of different ways (Henderson & Mapp, 2002; Mapp, 2003). Further, studies of immigrant Latino, African American, and other underrepresented family groups have repeatedly found that they are "highly interested" in being more directly involved (Trumbull et al., 2001, p. 32). Ramos (2014) reported that Latina mothers supported their children's education through typical forms of engagement (i.e., reading to their children, volunteering in the classroom, attending parent–teacher meeting, etc.), but they also engaged in cultural forms of parental engagement, which extended beyond the typical forms of engagement. In reviewing the Latina mothers' responses, Ramos revealed that three themes regarding culturally embedded parental engagement emerged:

> *sacrificios, consejos,* and *apoyo. Sacrificios* refers to a mental state of struggle and sacrifice in the interest of enhancing or supporting children's education and learning. . . . Mothers delighted in the thought of their *sacrificios* motivating their children finish school and to be "somebody" in the future. . . . *Consejos* refers to advice parents give their young children about school that reinforces values, such as resiliency and perseverance . . . mothers' plea that children should not "be like me, but be better" and that education was a means to accomplish this. . . . *Apoyo* refers to the emotional and moral support parents offer their children to boost their self-esteem and encourage their perseverance so that they do well in school . . . a mother of a five-year-old [girl said] . . . "I give her praise, hugs and kisses. And I tell her that she is smart." (pp. 3–5)

In an earlier study, Anderson and Stokes (1984) observed families from Anglo American, Black American, and Mexican American populations to determine the average frequency of literacy events per hour of observation. They identified nine "domains of literacy activity" including (1) religion, (2) daily living, (3) entertainment (source, instrumental, media), (4) school-related activity, (5) general information, (6) work, (7) literacy techniques and skills (adult-initiated, child-initiated), (8) interpersonal communication, and (9) storybook time. In contrast to the belief that many minority children do not begin school with rich literacy backgrounds, Anderson and Stokes found that minority children in their study had varied literacy experiences in several domains of literacy activity. They found that 26.5% of all literacy activity for the Black American population in their study fell into the category of religion, surpassed only by the entertainment category (30.2%).

In addition to learning the importance of religious-oriented literacy activities in the lives of some Black Americans, Anderson and Stokes discussed social institutional influences that religious activities had on literacy practices and beliefs. They found information contrary to the belief that Black and Mexican American families who practice religion are only engaged in "oral tradition." In fact, the churches that the families in their study attended, encouraged—and in some cases required—an active, assertive approach to print.

Rather than assuming families are unwilling to become more active partners with schools, educators would do well to examine closely the specific causes of poor school–family relationships and low levels of involvement in their community. By examining these barriers, schools can begin to develop solutions for gaining support and trust. Brewster and Railsback (2003) reveal some common obstacles and barriers to building strong family–school relationships (see Figure 7.1 at the end of this chapter, adapted from Brewster and Railsback). As a result, many parents may not become involved if they do not feel that the school climate—the social and educational atmosphere of the school—is one that makes them feel welcomed, respected, trusted, heard, and needed. A positive school climate welcomes and encourages family involvement.

As I have emphasized throughout this book, a critical first step in engaging families is to focus on building relationships of mutual trust, confidence, and respect. As Henderson and Mapp (2002) emphasize, "When outreach efforts reflect a sincere desire to engage parents and community members as partners in children's education, the studies show that they respond positively" (p. 66). Brewster and Railsback (2003) suggest some strategies for building trust between families and schools (see Figure 7.2 at the end of this chapter, which summarizes many of the points made throughout this book).

INVITE FAMILIES INTO SCHOOLS

An important early step in establishing effective school–parent relationships, according to Purkey and Novak (1984), is for schools and school professionals to work at making schools "the most inviting place in town" (p. 2). Purkey and Novak recommend four principles of invitational education: (1) treating people in ways that recognize them as able, valuable, and responsible; (2) teaching as a cooperative activity; (3) viewing people as possessing relatively untapped potential in all areas of human development; and (4) working to make school places, policies, and programs that are specifically designed to invite development, with school professionals who are personally and professionally inviting (p. 2).

Henderson, Marburger, and Ooms (1986) define "family-friendly schools as those that create a climate in which every aspect of the school is open and helpful" (p. 27). Family-friendly schools strive to forge partnerships with *all* families, not just those that are already most involved. Family-friendly schools incorporate strategies that reach out to all families and help involve them in their children's education. Family-friendly schools help to make sure that the school is a place where families and community members feel welcomed, informed, and included. Ballen and Moles (1994) believe that schools must become places where families feel wanted and recognized for their strengths and potential. Leuder (1998) suggests that schools should convey to parents that "you are welcome, you are important to us, and we want to work with you to educate your children" (p. 62). At Morton Professional Development School, a strategy I employed was parent informant meetings, as discussed in Chapter 5. Hoover-Dempsey et al. (2005) provide some other strategies for creating an inviting, welcoming school climate:

- Create visual displays in school entry areas and hallways reflective of all families in the school (photos, artifacts, pictures, history); focus on creating a strong sense that "this is *our* school; *we* belong here."
- Attend to the critical role of central factors in the creation of positive school climate: principal leadership; long-term commitment to improving and maintaining a positive school climate; creation of trust through mutually respectful, responsive, and communicative teacher–parent relationships.
- Develop strong, positive office-staff skills with a consumer orientation; create habitual attitudes of respect toward parents, students, and visitors.
- Create multiple comfortable spaces for parents in the school, supportive of parent–teacher conversations and parent networking.
- Hire parents or seek parent volunteers who can provide other parents with information on how the school works, translations as needed, advocacy as needed, a friendly presence.
- Offer *specific* invitations to specific events and volunteer opportunities at school; schedule activities at times that meet the needs of families with inflexible work schedules. (Hoover-Dempsey et al., 2005, p. 118)

The first step in building family-friendly schools is to investigate the school's historical family-involvement policies and practices.

Historical connections between homes and schools can affect families' involvement in schools. Today's school personnel must closely examine their school's history to determine whether past policies and practices made parents feel invited or uninvited.

CLOSING COMMENTS

Making schools inviting spaces where parents and families are not only welcomed but actively engaged seems more challenging in the diverse, heterogeneous schools and communities of 21st-century America. It is my belief, however, that if school leaders and teachers take seriously their responsibility to provide a high-quality education for all students, they must work to "substantially change the structures, roles, and relationships within the schools . . . [and] the nature and distribution of power among schools, families, and communities" (Lightfoot, 1980, p. 17). In order to do this, they must first work to understand the ghosts of the past that continue to haunt family–school relationships in their communities and then work actively to invite and empower parents as collaborators in children's education.

Figure 7.1. Barriers and Obstacles to Building Strong Family–School Partnerships

---

Bad First Impressions

The way parents and other family members are received the first time they come to the school can set the tone for the duration of their relationship. Families who feel ignored or slighted by the adults in the building are unlikely to come back, especially if they had been hesitant to come to the school in the first place.

Poor Communication

Whether it is miscommunication or a lack of communication on the part of both families and schools, these issues can create tension and distrust.

Past Experiences

Family members' prior experiences with school also have a significant impact on how willing they are to trust school staff members and become involved in their children's schooling (Antunez, 2000; Mapp, 2003). Family members whose own experiences were negative may not feel comfortable entering the school building or may not trust that teachers will value their input. Similarly, families who have encountered problems with another teacher or with another school their child attended may question the value of communicating with schools at all. Teachers, too, who have had previous negative experiences with families may question the value of communicating with others.

Family Members' Lack of Self-Confidence

Some may not believe that they are capable of contributing to their children's education (Antunez, 2000); others find school personnel intimidating and fear looking incompetent if they ask teachers questions about how to help. Families may doubt that they have anything to offer by participating in the classroom, working with their children on schoolwork at home, or serving on school decisionmaking teams (Trumbull et al., 2001).

Teachers' Lack of Confidence

An equally powerful barrier to developing strong relationships with families is teachers' lack of confidence. According to Hoover-Dempsey (as cited in Onikama, Hammond, & Koki, 1998, p. 7), "a teacher's belief in his or her own teaching effectiveness is the strongest predictor of successful parent involvement." Newer teachers, in particular, may fear being viewed as incompetent by family members and thus initially avoid contact with them. New and veteran teachers alike may also doubt their ability to involve families effectively (Onikama et al., 1998). Until recently, few teacher programs offered training on working with families as partners in their children's education (Edwards, 2004). Even fewer addressed strategies for collaborating with families from diverse cultural, linguistic, and socioeconomic backgrounds (Edwards, 2004).

Figure 7.1. Barriers and Obstacles to Building Strong Family–School Partnerships (continued)

History of Discrimination

Past and present acts of discrimination—whether they occurred in school or in the larger community—remain a major barrier to family involvement and trust in schools (Antunez, 2000; Edwards, 2004). As Onikama et al. (1998) emphasize, "It is difficult for families to want to become involved with institutions they perceived are 'owned' by a culture that discriminated against them in the past" (p. 5).

Differing Expectations of Parent–Teacher Roles

Recent immigrants to the United States may have little knowledge of the public school system, much less a particular district's expectations regarding family involvement in their child's education. They may also hold very different beliefs about the roles of teachers and parents than those assumed at school (Trumbull et al., 2001). As Antunez (2000) notes,

> In some cultures . . . teaming with the school is not a tradition. Education has been historically perceived as the responsibility of the schools, and family intervention is viewed as interference with what trained professionals are supposed to do. (p. 55)

Families from such cultures may believe that their role is to raise "respectful, well-behaved beings" and leave the academic instruction to schools (Trumbull et al., 2001, p. 39).

Lack of Confidence in the School

Families' doubts about school effectiveness, teacher competence, and the integrity of school leaders are prime causes of mistrust and unwillingness to engage in activities related to the school. Family members who raise concerns about a problem at school and fail to see any action may see no reason to continue interacting with the staff. Persistent problems, such as low test scores or repeated incidents of violence and discrimination, may lead some to conclude that educators simply are not doing their job. As many districts have seen, negative news coverage can exacerbate this problem, especially if it is the only source of information families and other community members receive about teachers, school leaders, and school performance.

Note. Adapted from Brewster and Railsback, 2003.

Figure 7.2. Strategies for Building Trust Between Families and Schools

Assess the Level of Trust in the School Community

Selecting an assessment tool is a good place to start (e.g., see Resource 7.1, "Family-Friendly School Parent Survey," tcpress.com). Discuss perceptions of current school–family relationships with teachers, administrators, students, parents, and other family members; identify specific barriers to trust in your community; and solicit input from all parties on ways to address them.

Actively Welcome Students and Families

Letting families know that they are welcome in the school building, greeting them when they arrive, and posting signs in their native language are just a few ways to communicate to parents that they are valued members of the school community. Hiring administrative staff who speak the same language as families is another way not only to welcome bilingual families but to provide them with someone who can act as an interpreter. Parents and other family members are also more likely to trust that the school values their involvement when they see people who share their cultural and linguistic background among the school staff.

Begin Relationship on a Positive Note

Adams and Christenson (2000) remark that often,

> the only time parents have contact with the school is in crisis situations such as when the student violated school regulations . . . with no previous contact . . . these situations often lead to nontrusting interactions and, subsequently, non-optimal results for the student. A previous time in which to signal trusting intentions is considered an essential prerequisite for handling critical issues for students. (p. 482)

Teachers whose first contacts with family members are positive—notes or phone calls about something good the student did in class, for example—demonstrate to families that the school is interested in and values their child.

Highlight School Successes

Families cannot be expected to place trust in schools and teachers about whom they know very little. Identify ways to communicate with parents and other family members about student accomplishments, professional development efforts, and other school programs that reflect the school's commitment to high-quality teaching and learning.

Improve School–Family Communication

Too often, school–home communication is only one-way, with schools determining what information parents need and sending it to them. Opening up more and better ways for families to communicate with schools, listening to what they say, and responding seriously are essential to trust-building (Adams & Christenson, 2000). "Make sure that you convey the message to parents that their input is considered valuable" (Voltz, 1994, p. 290).

Figure 7.2. Strategies for Building Trust Between Families and Schools (continued)

Demonstrate That You Care

Knowing that principals, teachers, and other school staff have their children's best interests at heart is critical to families' developing trust in schools (Goddard et al., 2001). Even small things, such as learning a few words in a family's native language, make a difference.

Show Respect for All Families

Voltz (1994) advises educators to use titles, such as Mr., Ms., or Mrs., when addressing parents, unless they tell you otherwise: "Although the use of first names in some may be viewed as a means of establishing a collegial, friendly relationship, in other cultures, it is viewed as disrespectful or forward" (p. 290). Using a "tone of voice that expresses courtesy and respect" (Brewster & Railsback, 2003, p. 20) is also important.

Treat Parents as Individuals

"Resist the stereotyping of parents based on race, ethnicity, socioeconomic status, or any other characteristic. Recognize the diversity that occurs within cultural groups, as well as that which occurs between them" (Voltz, 1994, p. 290).

Be Open with Parents

As Voltz (1994) advises, "Don't ignore or dodge tough issues" (p. 290). Making information easily accessible to families, providing it in language they can understand, and ensuring that they know whom to talk to if they have questions is a good place to start in demonstrating openness.

Take Parents' Concerns Seriously

Listen, respond, and follow through. Depending on the situation, consider inviting families to help generate solutions. Be sure that they know what is being done to address their concerns.

Promote Professionalism and Strong Teaching

To build strong family–school trust, families must view the school principal, teachers, and other personnel as competent, honest, and reliable. Failure to remove staff members who are widely viewed to be racist or ineffective, according to Bryk and Schneider (2002), quickly leads to low levels of trust in the school and its leadership.

Remember That Trust-Building Takes Time

Families whose past encounters with the school or community have been negative may have no reason to expect things will be different now. Rebuilding trust takes time and a serious commitment to establishing strong relationships:

> When a school initiates and implements programs, policies, and procedures with the express intention of seriously meeting the needs of the students, then the school can begin to develop an environment in which the community can begin to rightfully place trust in the local school and its staff. (Young, 1998, p. 18)

Note. Adapted from Brewster and Railsback, 2003.

CHAPTER 8

A New Vision— Seeing More Clearly

> Families . . . are the most important visitors on our premises. They are not dependent on us, we are dependent on them. They are not outsiders in our business, they are part of it. We are not doing them a favor by serving them, they are doing us a favor.
>
> —Florida Partnership for Family Involvement in Education, *Opening Doors*

Throughout this book, I have emphasized that to involve *all* parents, schools in the 21st century need to be open and friendly places for a diverse group of families. Educators should play a key role in this process by encouraging parents to participate in a variety of ways. Meaningful parent involvement can only be achieved when the school does the following:

- Reaches out to parents in new ways
- Helps parents connect to resources
- Creates an environment that makes parents feel welcome
- Provides numerous opportunities for participation

Family and community involvement is an essential component of a successful school program—along with curriculum, instruction, assessment, and other aspects of regular school life. Good communication and relationships among schools, families, and communities help maximize students' chances of success (Epstein, 2011; Henderson & Mapp, 2002; Jeynes, 2005).

Over 20 years ago, Shields (1994) argued that this vision of school improvement compels us to create a new conception of the appropriate relationship between the school and its community, parents, and families. Pedagogically, as we have come to know the importance of rooting learning in children's real lives, we can no longer tolerate the artificial boundaries between the classroom and the home. Politically, as we move the authority for decisionmaking down to those closest to children, we cannot afford to exclude parents and community members from the process of crafting new schools. Nor can we avoid being held more directly accountable to the immediate community constituency for decisions made at the school site. Practically, schools have no chance of enacting fundamental changes on the reform agenda in the absence of wholehearted support from their entire community—parents, citizens, and businesses.

The idea that schools can best succeed by isolating themselves and their students from the community has been discredited (Epstein, 2001, 2011; Sheridan & Kratochwill, 2007). In the second decade of the 21st century, the improvement of our schools will have to be accompanied by closer connections between schools and their communities, teachers, and families. In this closing chapter, I describe some models for creating a new vision for parent involvement that draw on points made throughout this book.

MODELS OF PARENT INVOLVEMENT

Joyce Epstein (2001, 2011) is one of the most frequently cited authors when it comes to theorizing about parental involvement. In Epstein's opinion, schools and families share responsibilities for the socialization of the child. Therefore, her theory of overlapping spheres of influence posits that the work of the most effective families and schools overlaps as they share goals and missions. There are three most important contexts in which children grow and develop: family, school, and community. Although some practices of school and family are conducted separately, there are some important things that need to be done conjointly, reflecting the shared responsibilities of parents and educators. Epstein (2001) proposed a framework of parent involvement that includes six main types of activities that connect families, schools, and communities:

- *Parenting* includes the basic childrearing approaches that prepare children for school.
- *Communicating* includes effective forms of both home-to-school and school-to-home information sharing about school programs as well as children's progress.

- *Volunteering* may involve parents who work at the school level, assisting teachers in classrooms. It may also include parental support for their children in extracurricular activities such as sports and other events.
- *Learning at home* includes "requests and guidance from teachers for parents to assist their own children at home on learning activities that are coordinated with the children's class work" (p. 136).
- *Participating in decisionmaking* includes families in school governance and advocacy through school advisory councils, PTA, and other groups that support and develop parents as leaders and representatives.
- *Collaborating with the community* engages parents in identifying relevant community resources and helping to integrate them in ways that support children's learning and strengthen school programs.

Although these are some recommendations that can be drawn from Epstein's work, she warns that there is no cookie-cutter set of programs or approaches that will work for all schools or for all family and community members. This means that parent involvement would look different in different schools, as individual schools tailor their practices to meet the specific needs of students and their families.

Family–school partnership is a perspective that can be used in a comprehensive analysis of various factors influencing and promoting overall child development, primarily focusing on the interweaving roles of two key agents in education and socialization: family and school. Analyzing the facets of this partnership and the ways for promoting it, Sheridan and Kratochwill (2007) point out the key differences between the partnership approach and the traditional way of conceptualizing family–school relations. These differences are outlined in Figure 8.1.

The defining characteristics of the family–school partnership are presented in Figure 8.2. Sheridan and Kratochwill (2007) put special stress on two of them: collaborative relationships and shared responsibility for the educational outcomes.

In a collaborative approach to schooling, issues between the family and the school are defined primarily by trust, which opens the door to transparent and sincere communication and supports consensual decisionmaking. Only if both of the partners see each other as equal can their efforts jointly contribute to the best outcomes for children.

Figure 8.1. The Differences Between Traditional and Partnership Orientation

Partnership Orientation	Traditional Orientation
Clear commitment to work together in order to promote child's performance/achievement	Emphasizing the school role in promoting learning
Frequent communication that is bidirectional	Communication initiated just by the school, infrequent and problem-centered
Appreciating the cultural differences and recognizing the importance of their contribution to creating the positive learning climate	"One size fits all"—cultural difference is a challenge that needs to be overcome
Appreciation of the significance of different perspectives	Differences are seen as barriers
Roles are clear, mutual, and supportive	Separate roles distance participants
Goals for students are mutually determined and shared	Goals determined by school, sometimes shared with parents
Plans are co-constructed with agreed-upon roles for all participants	Educational plans devised and delivered by teachers

Source: Sheridan & Kratochwill (2007). Reprinted by permission of Springer Science+Business Media.

Shared responsibility is completely absent in the traditional perspective, which is actually the operating principle in the majority of schools. Blaming just the school or just the family for a child's failure does not promote the partnership but prevents it from developing in complementary ways. Sheridan and Kratochwill (2007) point to a few theories underlying the concept of partnership—including ecological theory, behavioral theory, and the family-centered approach—and then describe a shift toward a partnership-centered approach.

Ecological theory is concerned with the multiple interdependent, inseparable systems or environments and contexts that surround children's development and education:

- Microsystems: home, classroom
- Mesosystems: the interrelation of microsystems
- Exosystems: influencing the microsystems—for example, parents' working environment that supports parental involvement or produces various obstacles for it
- Macrosystems: overall societal and cultural setting, including national educational policies

Figure 8.2. Defining Characteristics of the Family–School Partnership

Characteristics	Key Indicators
Relationships among partners are *collaborative, interdependent,* and *balanced*	• Diverse individuals and vantage points work together as coequal parties, share in the identification of goals and solutions of problems, and forge trusting relationships. • More than simply working together, the notion of partnerships involves a fundamental restructuring of how individuals work together across home and school systems. • Roles are complementary—each partner makes a unique contribution that is mutually beneficial. • All have generally equal opportunity in decisionmaking.
Responsibility for educating and socializing children is shared	• Resources, power, and responsibilities are shared. • Goals are mutually determined. • Outcomes achieved in the context of the partnership are uniquely superior to those achieved by any one party in isolation.
Maintenance of a positive relationship is a priority	• Failure to develop relationships can undermine the formation of successful partnerships. • Personal needs are put aside to allow the needs and goals of the partnership to take precedence. • To be successful, partners must believe that the other person is trustworthy, is working toward a mutually held goal, and holds positive regard toward the other. • All believe that the partnership and the anticipated outcomes are worthy of the expenditure of time and energy necessary for its maintenance.
Services are flexible, responsive, and proactive	• Unique family–school contexts define the form the partnership takes.
Differences in perspectives are seen as strengths	• A range of diverse experiences, skills, and views are brought to bear on the solution of problems. • Unique knowledge, resources, talents, and expertise brought by parents and educators enhance the potential outcomes for students.
There is a commitment to cultural competence	• Cultural values and traditions of the family and school are respected. • Services that are sensitive to important cultures and traditions of schools and families are most likely to be effective.
Emphasis is on outcomes and goal attainment	• Partnerships have clearly specified goals, and progress is monitored through data-based decisionmaking processes. • Programs are not offered because they are available; rather, they are considered fully with attention to the degree to which they fit within the overarching priorities of the partnership.

Source: Sheridan & Kratochwill (2007). Reprinted by permission of Springer Science+Business Media.

The key input taken from this theory is the importance of meso-system, the interaction of the two most important microsystems in education. Behavioral theory is important because it stresses the importance of learning and focuses on the "here and now" of the situation—identifying the environmental (in contrast to personal, dispositional) factors that influence the family–school interaction. Sheridan and Kratochwill's (2007) approach is therefore ecological-behavioral, blending the strengths of both approaches: paying attention to behavior but having in mind the systematic influences of the interweaving environments. The authors go beyond these two approaches, including family-centered services, since empowering and strengthening the family is necessary for an effective partnership. Therefore, in order to form such a partnership between the school and the family, it is important to identify needs, mobilize the resources, and accomplish goals through the development of family capacities, strengths, and abilities.

From a partnership-centered orientation, Sheridan and Kratochwill (2007) pay special attention to the development of skills and competencies of both family members and educators. Important steps in this process include the following:

- Creating meaningful roles for family members in supporting their child's learning
- Promoting continuity
- Enhancing competencies of all participants

Continuity across home and school is important because it supports effective learning transitions. Sheridan and Kratochwill (2007) cite the results of an ethnographic study that had shown that low-achieving adolescent students often reported a discontinuity between the family, school, and peers when it comes to, for example, valuing aspects of culture such as values, beliefs, knowledge, and skills. Phelan, Davidson, and Yu (1998) found that the lack of this type of congruence within the child–family–school system significantly influenced academic achievement.

A PARADIGM SHIFT

Many equate parent engagement with volunteering, school governance, and fundraising. While these activities are vitally important to schools, the kind of parent engagement that affects student success is vastly different. This type of engagement involves parents as teachers and learners. It means building parent–school partnerships that not only increase student learning but expand learning for everyone in a child's support system. Teachers and other school professionals must learn about elements of the home and community culture, and likewise, family and community members must learn about key elements of school culture in order to work toward congruence in their everyday lives. In this type of partnership, everyone is mobilized to learn in order to better support the child's learning and development.

Today's concept of family–school partnerships echoes back to the ideas of Ira Gordon (1977), who implied that parents and schools share equally valued roles in education. To make partnerships flourish, we must go beyond thinking of parents as school volunteers and fundraisers and consider them part of a school's learning community.

Instead of a closed, self-sufficient system, schools must see themselves as open systems that engage in learning at the boundaries between families and communities. Peter Senge (2000) said it well:

> If I had one wish for all our institutions, and the institution called school in particular, it is that we dedicate ourselves to allowing them to be what they would naturally become, which is human communities, not machines. Living beings who continually ask the questions: Why am I here? What is going on in my world? How might I and we best contribute? (p. 60)

When we think of schools as learning communities, parents and teachers have the capacity to shift the machine metaphor from the grassroots upward. This is the type of change than cannot be mandated from the top down or through policies like No Child Left Behind and the Common Core State Standards. In fact, research shows that partnerships based on relationships, connectedness, and flexibility hold the keys to understanding how to increase student learning and motivation.

What does this paradigm shift mean to families and schools? While parents and teachers have unique skills and expertise, no one is a single expert. We are all learners. We come together for the shared goal of educating the whole child. In many ways, we are what Wenger, McDermott, and Snyder (2002) call *communities of practice*—"groups of people who share a concern, a set of problems, or a passion about a topic, and who deepen their understanding and knowledge of this area by interacting on an ongoing basis" (p. 4). What brings families and schools together is a passion for children and education.

CLOSING COMMENTS

Best practice indicates that student success hinges on teachers and administrators who welcome parents into schools and encourage and assist them with the means by which to help their children to succeed. No longer is it feasible for parents to remain on the sidelines because they may not see themselves as instrumental in educating their children. No longer is it acceptable for teachers to leave parents on the periphery of instruction. Teachers and administrators have the power to encourage and assist toward the goal of making a comforting and welcoming environment for parents. It is important to observe and play on the strengths that parents bring to schools and to make certain that parents recognize that they are important to the education of their children. In order to create an inviting environment, it is imperative that teachers and administrators work together to find the best ways in which to welcome parents into their schools.

A new vision of parental involvement centrally acknowledges families' important role in the school community. The family–school partnership perspective suggests that acknowledging parents' shared responsibility in education, offering multiple and varied opportunities for parents to participate, leveraging parents' strengths, and matching supports to parents can help parents become involved in their children's schooling. A vision of families and schools as partners in the educational process is one that needs to move from vision to reality for the benefit of students for whom families and schools share aspirations and responsibilities.

References

Adams, K. S., & Christenson, S. L. (2000). Trust and the family–school relationship: Examination of parent–teacher differences in elementary and secondary grades. *Journal of School Psychology, 38*(5), 477–497.

Allen, J. (2010). *Literacy in the welcoming classroom: Creating family–school partnerships that support student learning.* New York, NY: Teachers College Press.

Allen, J., Shockley, B., & Michalove, B. (1995). *Connecting home and school literacy communities.* Portsmouth, NH: Heinemann.

Anderson, A. B., & Stokes, S. J. (1984). Social and institutional influences on the development and practice of literacy. In H. Goelman, A. Oberg, & F. Smith (Eds.), *Awakening to literacy* (pp. 24–37). Exeter, NH: Heinemann.

Antunez, B. (2000). When everyone is involved: Parents and communities in school reform. In B. Antunez, P. A. DiCerbo, & K. Menken, *Framing effective practice: Topics and issues in the education of English language learners* (pp. 53–59). Washington, DC: National Clearinghouse for Bilingual Education.

Ascher, C. (1988). Improving the school–home connection for poor and minority urban students. *The Urban Review, 20*(2), 109–123.

Ballen, J., & Moles, O. (1994). *Strong families, strong schools.* Washington, DC: U.S. Department of Education.

Barnett, S. W. (2002). Preschool education for economically disadvantaged children: Effects on reading achievement and related outcomes. In S. B. Neuman & D. K. Dickinson (Eds.), *Handbook of early literacy research* (pp. 421–443). New York, NY: Guilford.

Bennett, C. I. (1999). *Comprehensive multicultural education: Theory and practice* (4th ed.). Boston, MA: Allyn & Bacon.

Berger, E. H. (1991). *Parents as partners in education: The school and home working together* (3rd ed.). New York, NY: Merrill.

Berger, E. H. (1995). *Parents as partners in education: Families and schools working together* (4th ed.). New York, NY: Merrill.

Berger, E. H. (2000). *Parents as partners in education.* Upper Saddle River, NJ: Merrill Prentice Hall.

Berliner, D. (1986). Does culture affect reading comprehension? *Instructor, 96*(3), 28–29.

Billingsley, A. (1968). *Black families in White America.* Englewood Cliffs, NJ: Prentice-Hall.

Boethel, M. (2003). *Diversity: School, family and community connections with schools*. Austin, TX: Southwest Educational Development Laboratory.

Brewer, W. R., & Kallick, B. (1996). Technology's promise for reporting student learning. In T. R. Guskey (Ed.), *Communicating student learning: 1996 ASCD yearbook* (pp. 178–187). Alexandria, VA: Association for Supervision and Curriculum Development.

Brewster, C., & Railsback, J. (2003). *Building trust with schools and diverse families: A foundation for lasting partnerships.* Retrieved from www.google .com/?gws_rd=ssl#q=building+trust+with+schools+and+diverse+families

Broatch, L. (2014). 10 good reasons your child should attend preschool. Retrieved from www.greatschools.org/students/academic-skills/1113-why -preschool.gs

Brown v. Topeka Board of Education, 347 U.S. 483, 1954.

Bryk, A. S., & Schneider, B. (2002). *Trust in schools: A core resource for improvement.* New York, NY: Russell Sage Foundation.

Burke, R. (1999). Diverse family structures: Implications for P–3 teachers. *Journal of Early Childhood Teacher Education, 20,* 245–251.

Carson, B. (with Murphey, C.). (1990). *Gifted hands: The Ben Carson story.* Grand Rapids, MI: Zondervan.

Christian, S. (2009). *Children of incarcerated parents.* Retrieved from www.f2f. ca.gov/res/pdf/ChildrenOfIncarceratedParents2.pdf

Clemens-Brower, T. J. (1997). Recruiting parents and the community. *Educational Leadership, 54*(5), 58–60.

Colorín Colorado. (2007). *Empowering ELL parents & families at home.* Retrieved from www.colorincolorado.org/article/14313/

Comer, J. P. (1988). *Maggie's American dream: The life and times of a Black family.* New York, NY: Penguin Books.

Comer, J. P. (1990). Home, school, and academic learning. In J. L. Goodlad & P. Keating (Eds.), *Access to knowledge: An agenda for our nation's schools* (pp. 23–42). New York, NY: College Entrance Board.

Compton-Lilly, C. (2009). Listening to families over time: Seven lessons learned about literacy in families. *Language Arts, 86,* 449–457.

Crouch, R. (2012). The United States of education: The changing demographics of the United States and their schools. Retrieved from www .centerforpubliceducation.org/You-May-Also-Be-Interested-In-landing -page-level/Organizing-a-School-YMABI/The-United-States-of -education-The-changing-demographics-of-the-United-States-and -their-schools.html

Delpit, L. (1988). The silenced dialogue: Power and pedagogy in educating other people's children. *Harvard Education Review, 58,* 280–298.

Derman-Sparks, L., & Edwards, J. O. (2010). *Anti-bias education for young children and ourselves.* Washington, DC: National Association for the Education of Young Children.

Dewey, J. (1902). *The child and the curriculum.* Chicago, IL: University of Chicago.

Diamond, J. B., & Moore, M. (1995). *Mirroring the new reality of the classroom: A multicultural literacy approach.* White Plains, NY: Longman.

Dickinson, D. K., McCabe, A., & Essex, M. J. (2006). A window of opportunity we must open to all: The case for preschool with high-quality support for language and literacy. In D. K. Dickinson & S. B. Neuman (Eds.), *Handbook of early literacy research* (Vol. 2, pp. 11–28). New York, NY: Guilford.

Du Bois, W. E. B. (1903). *The souls of Black folk.* New York, NY: Bantam Classic.

Edwards, P. A. (1990). *Parents as partners in reading: A family literacy training program.* Chicago, IL: Children's Press.

Edwards, P. A. (1992). Involving parents in building reading instruction for African-American children. *Theory Into Practice, 31*(4), 350–359.

Edwards, P. A. (1993a). Before and after school desegregation: African-American parent involvement in schools. *Educational Policy: An Interdisciplinary Journal of Policy and Practice, 7*(3), 340–369.

Edwards, P. A. (1993b). *Parents as partners in reading: A family literacy training program* (2nd ed.). Chicago, IL: Children's Press.

Edwards, P. A. (1995). Combining parents' and teachers' thoughts about storybook reading at home and school. In L. M. Morrow (Ed.), *Family literacy: Multiple perspectives to enhance literacy development* (pp. 54–60). Newark, DE: International Reading Association.

Edwards, P. A. (2004). *Children's literacy development: Making it happen through school, family, and community involvement.* Boston, MA: Allyn & Bacon.

Edwards, P. A. (2009). *Tapping the potential of parents: A strategic guide to boosting student achievement through family involvement.* New York, NY: Scholastic.

Edwards, P. A., McMillon, G. M. T., & Turner, J. D. (2010). *Change is gonna come: Transforming literacy education for African American children.* New York, NY: Teachers College Press.

Edwards, P. A., & Young, L. S. (1992). Beyond parents: Family, community, and school involvement. *Phi Delta Kappan, 74*(1), 72–80.

Epstein, J. L. (1988). How do we improve programs for parent involvement? *Educational Horizons, 66*(2), 58–59.

Epstein, J. L. (2001). *School, family, and community partnerships: Preparing educators and improving schools.* Boulder, CO: Westview Press.

Epstein, J. L. (2011). *School, family, and community partnerships: Preparing educators and improving schools* (2nd ed.). Philadelphia, PA: Westview Press.

Farris, P. J., & Denner, M. (1991). Guiding illiterate parents in assisting their children in emergent literacy. *Reading Horizons, 32*(1), 63–72.

Feistritzer, C. E. (2011). *Profile of teachers in the U.S. 2011.* Washington, DC: National Center for Education Information.

Ferguson, C. (2005). *Reaching out to diverse populations: What can schools do to foster family-school connections?* Austin, TX: Southwest Educational Development Laboratory.

Ferrel, J. (2012). *Family engagement and children with disabilities: A resource guide for educators and parents.* Cambridge, MA: Harvard Family Research Project.

Flatley, D. (2009). The importance of involving parents. Retrieved from http://teaching.monster.com/benefits/articles/9120-the-importance-of-involving-parents?print=true

Fletcher, R. (1966). *The family and marriage in Britain.* Harmondsworth, England: Penguin.

Fraatz, J.M.B. (1987). *The politics of reading: Power, opportunity and prospects for change in America's public schools.* New York, NY: Teachers College Press.

Gadsden, V. L. (1993). Literacy, education, and identity among African-Americans: The communal nature of learning. *Urban Education, 27*(4), 352–369.

Ghezzi, P. (2014). Recruiting preschool parents. *PTO Today.* Retrieved from www.ptotoday.com/pto-today-articles/article/287-recruiting-preschool-parents

Goddard, R. D., Tschannen-Moran, M., & Hoy, W. K. (2001). A multilevel examination of the distribution and effects of teacher trust in students and parents in urban elementary schools. *Elementary School Journal, 10*(2), 3–17.

Gordon, I. J. (1977). Parent education and parent involvement: Retrospect and prospect. *Childhood Education, 54,* 71–79.

Gordon, I. J. (1979). The effects of parent involvement on schooling. In R. S. Brandt (Ed.), *Partners: Parents and schools* (pp. 4–25). Alexandria, VA: Association for Supervision and Curriculum and Development.

Gormley, W., Gayer, T., Phillips, D. A., & Dawson, B. (2005). The effects of universal pre-K on cognitive development. *Developmental Psychology, 41,* 872–884.

Harrington, A. (1971). Teaching parents to help at home. In C. B. Smith (Ed.), *Parents and reading* (pp. 49–56). Newark, DE: International Reading Association.

Harvey, S., & Goudvis, A. (2007). *Strategies that work: Teaching comprehension for understanding and engagement* (2nd ed.). Portland, ME: Stenhouse.

Hawkins, L. (1970). Urban schoolteaching: The personal touch. In N. Wright, Jr. (Ed.), *What Black educators are saying* (pp. 43–47). New York, NY: Hawthorn Books.

Heath, S. B. (1989). Oral and literate traditions among Black Americans living in poverty. *American Psychologist, 44*(2), 367–373.

Henderson, A. T., & Mapp, K. L. (2002). *A new wave of evidence: The impact of school, family, and community connections on student achievement.* Austin, TX: Southwest Educational Development Laboratory. Retrieved from www.sedl.org/connections/resources/evidence.pdf

Henderson, A. T., Marburger, C. L., & Ooms, T. (1986). *Beyond the bake sale: An educator's guide to working with parents.* Columbia, MD: National Committee for Citizens in Education.

Henry, M. (1996). *Parent–school collaboration: Feminist organizational structures and school leadership*. Albany: State University of New York Press.

Hollins, E. R. (1996). *Culture in school learning: Revealing the deep meaning*. Mahwah, NJ: Erlbaum.

Hoover-Dempsey, K. V., & Whitaker, M. C. (2010). The parental involvement process: Implications for literacy development. In D. Fisher & K. Dunsmore (Eds.), *Bringing literacy home* (pp. 53–82). Newark, DE: International Reading Association.

Hoover-Dempsey, K. V., Walker, J. M. T., Sandler, H. M., Whetsel, D., Green, C. L., Wilkins, A. S., & Closson, K. (2005). Why do parents become involved? Research findings and implications. *Elementary School Journal, 106*(2), 105–130.

Howes, C., Burchinal, M., Pianta, R., Bryant, D., Early, D., Clifford, R., & Barbarin, O. (2008). Ready to learn? Children's pre-academic achievement in prekindergarten programs. *Early Childhood Research Quarterly, 23*, 27–50.

Hymes, J. L. (1974). *Effective home–school relations*. Whittier, CA: Southern California Association for the Education of Young Children.

Irvine, J. J. (1992). Making teacher education culturally responsive. In M. E. Dilworth (Ed.), *Diversity in teacher education: New expectations* (pp. 79–92). San Francisco, CA: Jossey-Bass.

Isaacs, J. (2013). *Unemployment from a child's perspective*. Washington, DC: The Urban Institute.

Jenkins, G. (1969). Understanding differences in parents. In N. Headley, H. Merhill, E. Mirbaha, & M. Rasmussen (Eds.), *Parents-children-teachers: Communication* (pp. 35–40). Washington, DC: Association for Childhood Education International.

Jeynes, W. H. (2005). A meta-analysis of the relation of parent involvement to urban elementary school student academic achievement. *Urban Education, 40*, 237–269.

Keene, E. O., & Zimmerman, S. (2007). *Mosaic of thought: The power of comprehension strategy instruction*. Portsmouth, NH: Heinemann.

Keyes, C. R. (2002). Parent–teacher partnerships: A theoretical approach for teachers. *International Journal of Early Years Education, 10*(3), 177–191.

Kost, K., Henshaw, S., & Carlin, L. (2010). *U.S. teenage pregnancies, births, and abortions: National and state trends and trends by race and ethnicity*. New York, NY: Guttmacher Institute. Retrieved from www.guttmacher.org/pubs/USTPtrends.pdf

Kreider, H., Mayer, E., & Vaughan, P. (1999). *Helping parents communicate better with schools*. Retrieved from colorincolorado.org/article/177/

Langdon, H. W., & Novak, J. M. (1998). Multicultures. *Educational HORIZONS, 77*, 15–17.

Leichter, H. (1984). Families as environments for literacy. In H. Goelman, A. Oberg, & F. Smith (Eds.), *Awakening to literacy* (pp. 38–50). Exeter, NH: Heinemann.

Lepi, K. (2013, March 20). 25 Twitter tips for students, parents, and teachers. *Edudemic*. Retrieved from www.edudemic.com/25-twitter-tips-for
-students-parents-and-teachers/

Leuder, D. C. (1998). *Creating partnerships with parents: An educator's guide*. Lan-
caster, PA: Technomic.

Li, G., Sweeney, J., Protacio, S., & Ponnan, M. (2013). A team training approach to professional development: Perceptions and practices of in-
service teachers of ELLs in two urban high schools. In Y. Bashevis & Y.
Weidenseid (Eds.), *Professional development: Perspectives, strategies, and practices* (pp. 37–56). Hauppauge, NY: Nova Science Publishers.

Lightfoot, S. L. (1978). *Worlds apart: Relationships between families and schools*.
New York, NY: Basic Books.

Lightfoot, S. L. (1980). Families as educators: The forgotten people of Brown.
In D. Bell (Ed.), *Shades of Brown: New perspectives on school desegregation* (pp.
3–19). New York, NY: Teachers College Press.

London Borough of Havering. (2013). *Working in partnership with parents: Good
practice guide*. London, England: Author. Retrieved from www.havering
.gov.uk/Documents/Children-young-people-and-families/Working-in
-Partnership-with-Parents-Good-Practice-Guide-2013.pdf

Mapp, K. L. (2003, Spring/Summer). Having their say: Parents describe why
and how they are engaged in their children's learning. *The School Community Journal, 13*(1), 35–64.

McLaughlin, M. W., & Shields, P. M. (1987). Involving low-income parents in
the schools: A role for policy? *Phi Delta Kappan, 69*, 156–160.

Moles, O. C. (1996, August). *Reaching all families: Creating family-friendly schools*.
Washington, DC: U.S. Department of Education Office of Educational Research and Improvement. Retrieved from www.ed.gov/pubs/ReachFam
/index.html

Morin, A. (2014). Questions to ask at parent teacher conferences: Parental involvement at parent teacher conferences. Retrieved from
childparenting.about.com/od/schoollearning/a/parent_teacher
_conference_questions_to_ask.htm

National Center for Education Statistics (NCES). (August, 2009). National Assessment of Educational Progress. Retrieved from nationsreportcard.gov

National PTA. (2000). *Building successful partnerships: A guide for development
parent and family involvement programs*. Bloomington, IN: National Educational Service.

Ogbu, J. U. (1995). Understanding cultural diversity and learning. In J. A.
Banks & C. A. Banks (Eds.), *Handbook on research in multicultural education*
(pp. 582–593). New York, NY: McMillan.

Onikama, D. L., Hammond, O. W., & Koki, S. (1998). *Family involvement in
education: A synthesis of research for Pacific educators*. Honolulu, HI: Pacific
Regional Educational Laboratory.

Phelan, P., Davidson, A. L., & Yu, H. C. (1998). *Adolescents' worlds: Negotiating family, peers, and school*. New York, NY: Teachers College Press.

Porter, A. (2012, July). Time for more parent accountability in nation's schools. Retrieved from www.washingtonpost.com/blogs/therootdc/post/time-for-more-parent-accountability-in-nations-schools/2012/07/30/gJQAE-JZaKX_blog.html

Potter, G. (1989). Parent participation in the language arts program. *Language Arts, 66*(1), 21–28.

Purkey, W. W., & Novak, J. M. (1984). *Inviting school success: A self-concept approach to teaching and learning*. Belmont, CA: Wadsworth.

Ramirez, F. (2001). Technology and parent involvement. *Clearinghouse, 75*(1), 274–278.

Ramos, M. (2014). *The strengths of Latina mothers in supporting their children's education: A cultural perspective*. Retrieved from www.childtrends.org/wp-content/uploads/2014/06/Strengths-of-Latinas-Mothers-formatted-6-10-14.pdf

Robinson, C. D. (2011, June 8). Holding parents accountable: Grades? Fines? Jail? *Washington Post*. Retrieved from www.washingtonpost.com/blogs/answer-sheet/post/holding-parents-accountable-grades-fines-jail/2011/06/07/AG0D4VLH_blog.html

Schiefflin, B. B., & Cochran-Smith, M. (1984). Learning to read culturally: Literacy before schooling. In H. Goelman, A. Oberg, & F. Smith (Eds.), *Awakening to literacy* (pp. 3–23). Exeter, NH: Heinemann.

Schussler, D. L. (2003). Schools as learning communities: Unpacking the concept. *Journal of School Leadership, 13*, 498–528.

SEDL National Center for Quality Afterschool. (2004–2009). Family literacy events. Retrieved from www.sedl.org/afterschool/toolkits/literacy/pr_family_literacy.html

Seeley, D. S. (1985). *Education through partnership*. Washington, DC: American Enterprise Institute for Public Policy Research.

Senge, P. M. (2000). Systems change in education. *Reflections, 1*(3), 52–60.

Shah, N. (2013). Parents' unemployment affects students at home, school. Retrieved from blogs.edweek.org/edweek/rulesforengagement/2013/03/parents_unemployment_affects_students_at_home_school.html

Sheridan, S. M., & Kratochwill, T. R. (2007). *Conjoint behavioral consultation: Promoting family–school connections and interventions*. New York, NY: Springer.

Shields, P. M. (1994). Bringing schools and communities together in preparation for the 21st century: Implications of the current educational reform movement for family and community involvement policies. Retrieved from www2.ed.gov/pubs/EdReformStudies/SysReforms/shields1.html

Springate, K. W., & Stegelin, D. A. (1999). *Building school and community partnerships through parent involvement*. Upper Saddle River, NJ: Prentice-Hall.

Stephens, G. E. (2013, August 15). *Cellphones, parents, and schools.* Retrieved from www.nassp.org/tabid/3788/defaultaspx?topic=Cellphones_Parents _and_Schools

Sweeney, J. (2012). *Veteran teachers working in diverse communities: Noticing students, families and communities* (Doctoral dissertation). Michigan State University, East Lansing. Retrieved from etd.lib.msu.edu/islandora/object /etd%3A295

Te Rito, B. (2011). *How to choose affordable equipment for making your online videos.* Retrieved from shetakesontheworld.com/2011/02/how-to -choose-affordable-equipment-for-making-your-online-videos/

Trumbull, E., Rothstein-Fisch, C., Greenfield, P. M., & Quiroz, B. (2001). *Bridging cultures between home and school: A guide for teachers.* Mahwah, NJ: Erlbaum.

U.S. Department of Education. (1999). *Start early, finish strong: How to help every child become a reader.* Washington, DC: Author.

Van Roekel, D. (2008). *An NEA policy brief: Parent, family, community involvement in education.* Washington, DC: National Education Association Education Policy and Practice Department.

Voltz, D. L. (1994). Developing collaborative parent–teacher relationships with culturally diverse parents. *Intervention in School & Clinic, 29*(5), 288–291.

Wenger, E., McDermott, R. A., & Snyder, W. (2002). *Cultivating communities of practice: A guide to managing knowledge.* Cambridge, MA: Harvard Business Press.

Wertsch, J. V. (1991). *Voices of the mind: A sociocultural approach to mediated action.* Cambridge, MA: Harvard University Press.

Young, M. D. (1998). *Importance of trust in increasing parental involvement and student achievement in Mexican American communities.* Paper presented at the Annual Meeting of the American Educational Research Association, San Diego, CA. Retrieved from files.eric.ed.gov/fulltext/ED423587.pdf

Zickuhr, K. (2011, February 3). *Generations and their gadgets.* Retrieved from the Pew Research Center website: www.pewinternet.org/2011/02/03 /generations-and-their-gadgets/

Index

About the Author

Patricia A. Edwards, member of the Reading Hall Fame, is a professor of language and literacy in the Department of Teacher Education at Michigan State University. She is a nationally and internationally recognized expert in parent involvement, home–school–community partnerships, multicultural literacy, early literacy, and family/intergenerational literacy, especially among poor and minority children. She has served as a member of the IRA board of directors (1998–2001), as the first African American president of the Literacy Research Association (2006–2007), and as president of the International Reading Association (2010–2011). She is the coauthor of *A Path to Follow: Learning to Listen to Parents* (1999, with Heather M. Pleasants and Sarah H. Franklin), *Bridging Literacy and Equity: The Essential Guide to Social Equity Teaching* (2012, with Althier M. Lazar and Gwendolyn T. McMillon), and *Change is Gonna Come: Transforming Literacy for African American Students* (2010, with Gwendolyn T. McMillon and Jennifer D. Turner). Dr. Edwards is also the author of *Tapping the Potential of Parents: A Strategic Guide to Boosting Student Achievement Through Family Involvement* (2009) and *Children Literacy Development: Making It Happen Through School, Family, and Community Involvement* (2004) and coeditor of *Best Practices in ELL Instruction* (2010, with Guofang Li). Dr. Edwards is the recipient of the Literacy Research Association's 2012 Albert J. Kingston Service Award, the International Reading Association's 2014 IRA Jerry Johns Outstanding Teacher Educator in Reading Award, and the 2015 Michigan Reading Association's Outstanding Teacher Educator Award.